D1137736

LEGAL PRACTICE HANDBOOK

EFFECTIVE

LEGAL PRACTICE HANDBOOK

EFFECTIVE INTERVIEWING

Helena Twist, LLM, FITD
Director of Legal Education,
Nabarro Nathanson, London

Series Editor: Anthony G. King, MA, Solicitor
Director of Education, Clifford Chance

BLACKSTONE
PRESS LIMITED

First published in Great Britain 1992 by Blackstone Press Limited,
9–15 Aldine Street, London W12 8AW. Telephone 081–740 1173

© H. Twist, 1992

ISBN: 1 85431 167 0

British Library Cataloguing in Publication Data
A CIP catalogue record for this book is available from the British
Library

Typeset by Style Photosetting Ltd, Mayfield, East Sussex
Printed by BPCC Wheatons Ltd, Exeter

Contents

For Joe

Acknowledgments

With special thanks to:

Jean and Kerry, for shouldering extra work and for tolerating my mood swings during the book's gestation.

Kay, Cora, Michelle and the Word Processing Department for typing or retyping my drafts.

My parents for their support.

All the clients I have ever interviewed and advised, for enabling me to learn a little more about human nature.

Introduction

In the course of your career you are likely to hear many conflicting views about developing good interviewing techniques. Some people argue that you need to be born with certain personality characteristics to be a good interviewer. Others maintain that it is enough simply to give potential interviewers a list of dos and don'ts and teach them how to apply that list. Still others argue that the skills of interviewing cannot be learned. This book takes the line that interviewing skills can be learned and improved.

Unless you understand something about clients' motivation, the nature of the communication process and how problems can arise, you will not find any list of dos and don'ts very helpful. A successful interviewer is someone who is aware of these issues, and has developed a repertory of skills and the ability to put them into practice. The skills are primarily concerned with creating the right climate for good communication between lawyer and client. Some people are good at creating an atmosphere in which communication flourishes. It may be that they are more sensitive, alert and interested in people. That awareness can be acquired. You can train yourself to listen more carefully, to observe more closely and to develop different questioning styles.

An interview is an interactional process. Both lawyer and client contribute to its success or failure, but the lawyer has greater power over, and therefore responsibility for, the process. An interview is sometimes described as 'a conversation with a purpose'. It is, in fact, a highly stylised form of conversation. In normal, everyday conversation, people generally exchange information and take it in turns to talk. In a legal interview you should expect the client to 'occupy' the interview and talk for at least 60 to 70 per cent of the time. Also the lawyer's role is principally to collect information, explore solutions, update on progress, advise and take action. It is not a true conversation.

Nevertheless the idea of the interview as a conversation means that, to an extent, we all come to interviewing with some experience of how to begin and how to behave. Interviews and meetings are a common experience of life. We understand that we have to listen and pay attention to what the other person is saying. Most of us have consulted doctors, been interviewed by professionals of one kind or another and been interviewed for a job. Some of these interviews or meetings will have proceeded smoothly and you will have felt comparatively at ease. You can probably also remember some unhappy or uncomfortable experiences.

Sometimes the expression 'meeting' is used to cover a whole range of face-to-face communications between lawyer and client, ranging from taking instructions, progress reviews and even negotiations. Good listening and questioning skills will assist you in these various situations. Understanding the factors which create a positive climate for communication, and how to handle difficult situations, will be an advantage in all types of professional meeting.

Equally, if your advice is being ignored, either in the first meeting or later in the relationship, for example, when you and your client are discussing how to progress a transaction, the techniques you can use, like acknowledging the client's interests or concerns, using questions to discover the causes for resistance and altering your body posture to a more 'controlling' one, apply whatever the forum.

It is important to avoid falling into the trap of assuming that clients who are articulate or successful are not subject to the same concerns as the rest of us about a case or matter proceeding well. Fundamentally, people are the same. When they consult a lawyer, it is because they need the lawyer's advice. If you are aware of their concerns and interests and give realistic commercial advice, your professional relationships should be successful.

In this book the expression 'lawyer' has been used deliberately. It can and should be interpreted to cover solicitors, barristers, trainees and pupils, legal executives and paralegals performing an interviewing role. If, in some places, the emphasis appears to be on taking instructions, it is because the first meeting can act as a microcosm of all the potential problems. If you can manage that meeting, then updating meetings and progress meetings will present no new or additional problems for you. The skills are transferable and can be used in a variety of situations.

Chapter One

Creating the Right Climate for Communication

1.1 BARRIERS AND BRIDGES TO EFFECTIVE COMMUNICATION

Generally clients go to see lawyers because they want a problem to be solved or averted. A large part of a lawyer's time is spent doing just that: attempting to resolve, overcome or avert problems. It would be reasonable to assume, then, that clients have an underlying motivation to participate fully in interviews and meetings. After all, they are looking for solutions, it is the lawyer's task to provide those solutions and they will want to give every assistance. Or will they? Communication difficulties can occur even when both parties want to cooperate.

This chapter looks at some of the potential barriers to good communication in the lawyer–client relationship. Some blocks to listening and poor questioning techniques are examined in greater detail in subsequent chapters. As a starting-point this chapter examines factors which can motivate clients to communicate, and behaviour and factors which can demotivate. A lawyer who is not alive to these may intuitively sense that all is not well, but not know how to unravel the problem. If you develop a mental checklist of potential problems you will be better able to manage the interview.

Creating the right atmosphere for discussion is not always easy. It cannot be done simply by an introductory statement like, 'How can I help?' It involves maintaining eye contact, listening and using reinforcing behaviour to show the client you are listening. A client who feels that the lawyer is paying attention is more likely to feel motivated to 'open up'. Conversely, a client who does not feel listened to may feel resentful, aggressive or unwilling to talk.

Interviews differ in the time and effort required. The total demands the interview makes on the client will also have a bearing on motivation. The greater the demands, the more the client needs to be encouraged. One of your tasks is to assess what demands are likely to be placed on the client and keep motivation at the right level for communication.

1.2 EMPATHY AND RAPPORT

It is your responsibility to establish a climate in which all the relevant issues can and will be discussed. This is particularly important when you are dealing with a client who has never visited a solicitor's office before, but it also applies to all your dealings with your clients. Taking time to establish rapport is essential. Although your clients are coming to see you for a particular reason, there may sometimes be some reserve or reluctance to talk, particularly if the problem involves personal issues. Creating the right climate entails you showing warmth, responsiveness and a real interest in the client.

Building empathetic relationships with your clients is an essential part of your role. Empathy is not the same as sympathy. Sympathy is experiencing the same emotion as someone else, or sharing that person's point of view. Empathy is the ability to understand another person's point of view or feelings. To be a successful interviewer, you do not have to sympathise with the client, but you do need to be able to listen and understand. Try to create a professional relationship with your clients which is open, receptive, committed and non-judgmental.

The relationship is a professional one, so do not assume that techniques which work in everyday social situations can be imported into the professional relationship. In social situations, people often use self-disclosure as a method of getting to know each other. They trade personal information, using expressions like, 'I know what you mean, when that happened to me . . .' to develop the relationship. Friendships are developed by this continual volunteering or reciprocity of personal information. Equally, if you do not wish to develop a relationship, you may choose to ignore information or not reciprocate.

Self-disclosure is not a suitable technique for establishing rapport with clients. Clients are generally not interested in the personal lives of their lawyers. If you talk about yourself for any length of time you will be intruding on your clients' time and they may feel impatient or frustrated. Keep your feelings, views and experiences out of the professional relationship, unless they have some professional relevance.

Physical and geographical factors can also have a bearing on the conduct of the interview. The seating arrangements and layout of the room, its temperature, state of tidiness or disarray, will all have an impact. This is also discussed in 4.4 and 6.5. If you are feeling tired, hung-over, or hungry, this will affect your concentration. If you allow telephone calls to interrupt your meeting with the client, that person may be made to feel unimportant and consequently may be less likely to communicate fully.

In the information-gathering interview, it is generally the lawyer who asks the questions and the client who gives the answers. Clumsily worded questions can cause problems. A question like 'Have you done what we agreed at our last meeting?' could have a negative effect. Whilst a confident or robust client will not be put off by this question, a client who has done nothing may feel embarrassed, at a disadvantage, or worse still, tempted not to answer truthfully.

1.3 LANGUAGE AND TERMINOLOGY

Language can enhance or hinder communication. If you use unfamiliar legal expressions or jargon, this will immediately inhibit communication. It could also cause misunderstandings. You should not assume that clients are familiar with legal terminology. Avoiding legal jargon does not mean talking down to clients; it means exercising consideration in your choice of words.

One definition of communication is 'the sharing of meaning'. Not sharing verbal meanings can cause all sorts of problems. If the client does not understand the terminology, the interview will not progress as well as it could. Lawyers have a large and specialised shared legal vocabulary. A corporate client or in-house lawyer will be well-versed in the terminology of their fields. A client going through a second divorce will have knowledge of the processes and legal language, but a new client may have little or no understanding. That client needs to be able to understand your meaning if you are going to work well together.

Consequently, the language of the interview should correspond with the shared vocabulary of the solicitor and client. A shared vocabulary does not mean that you both have to use the same colloquialisms and expressions, but rather that each of you can be understood by the other. Some clients may have preconceptions of how they expect their lawyers to behave and speak, based on what they have heard about lawyers. They may even come to the interview fearing being patronised or made to feel out of their depth. Make an effort to be understandable and approachable and avoid using words which confuse or bemuse clients.

When you use technical expressions, some clients may not know their meaning, so be sensitive to the need to explain. If you are discussing possible litigation with a client who has no experience of this process, rather than just referring to a statement of claim or pleadings, explain what these are in non-technical language. You can always use the technical expression later. Try giving an explanation before using the legal expression. That way you will find that your client is less likely to switch off and stop listening.

You should also consider increasing your own knowledge of your clients' vocabulary by making some effort to understand their business terminology, experiences and business concerns. Establishing rapport is a two-way process. Too often lawyers seem to think that their task is merely to explain and interpret the law to their clients. Unless you understand a client's business, you will not be able to give effective, commercial advice.

A lawyer's training is geared towards developing the ability to weigh evidence, evaluate and discriminate. This is a valuable skill for drafting or advocacy, but it can have a damaging effect on human interaction. Evaluative behaviour by the lawyer can distort or inhibit communication. If a client feels that the lawyer approves of a response, as evidenced by reinforcing behaviour like note-taking, head nods, or statements like, 'That's important', the client is likely to volunteer more of that kind of information. Similarly, if a client receives a negative signal in response to information, future disclosures of that type may be self-censored. You must learn to be very observant. Your responses and behaviour can sometimes unconsciously skew the relationship or distort the communication process.

1.4   EGO AND SELF-ESTEEM

A client may not want to reveal information which is ego threatening, which deals with difficult or delicate relationships or which involves feelings of guilt. Clients may be tempted to withhold the truth, or part of it, for fear of being shown in a bad light or as foolish or careless.

A client may also hold back information for fear of shocking or embarrassing you. This desire to protect you from the harsh realities of the real world can act as a barrier to communication. In divorce or child-abuse cases there is often a real reluctance to talk about unpleasant things. An older client faced with a young lawyer may find it difficult to bring these matters out into the open. A client may find it difficult to talk about sexual matters to a lawyer of the opposite sex. As a lawyer there will be times when you must identify and control these pressures and help the client.

The human desire for self-protection is not limited to embarrassing information. It can extend to not wishing to recall painful or traumatic memories. People naturally want to avoid situations which make them feel uncomfortable. It is your task to discover the relevant information and not allow clients to edit events or information.

Your own sense of self and confidence can have a positive or negative effect on client meetings. If you are feeling unconfident or unprepared, this can affect your concentration and act as a barrier to communication. The focus of your attention should be on your client – personal concerns should not intrude.

1.5   BRIDGES

Just as there are factors which can prevent or inhibit communication, there are things which you can do which actively assist communication.

All communication takes place within a context and this context influences the nature and effectiveness of that communication. Some of these influences have been discussed already. The business and interview context is fairly structured and formal. Your responsibility in the communication process is to take account of people's different attitudes and styles, that some people are more outgoing than others, some more assertive, others more placid, and still create the right climate for communication. The success of the interview rests to a large extent with your behaviour and how you approach your role.

1.5.1   Listening

For many clients, the experience of being listened to by a professional and receptive person is a relief. This sense of relief may encourage the client to disclose the relevant details. If you display 'helpful' behaviour and attentive listening, this will have a powerful and positive effect on the process and outcome.

1.5.2   Relief from anxiety

A client who is looking for real change, either in circumstances, or in the form of relief from an unpleasant state of affairs, is more likely to open up to the lawyer. If your clients see you as an agent for positive change, with special skills and knowledge at their disposal, your professional relationship is likely to be more effective.

1.5.3   Client's goals

Learning something about the client's goals may also facilitate communication. A client's desire to offer information may sometimes be affected by his or her goals. Take, for example, a consultation about a divorce where the lawyer asks the client about his home circumstances. If the client's wife is an alcoholic, it would be to the client's advantage to disclose this. In a different situation, if the client were trying to obtain advice on adoption, that client might decide initially to conceal this information for fear it could count against him, either with the lawyer or with the adoption agency.

1.5.4   Role conformity

Clothes and appearance have an effect on a relationship. A commercial lawyer, dressed for the part, might look out of place in a practice which wishes to project a different image. Role concept can also act as an important bridge in the interview. Positions in society or organisations carry with them certain expected ways of behaving. If you are a male lawyer in a City commercial practice, your firm will expect you to wear not only the right kind of suit, but to behave in a certain way. Your clients will also expect it. Conforming to social norms is a powerful bridge, so a lawyer who matches up to a client's expectations of appearance and behaviour will make that client feel more comfortable than the lawyer who does not.

You are not obliged to conform to clients' stereotypical views of lawyers, but fulfilling a client's expectations can help. The converse may also be true. Clients have their own expectations, both positive and negative, of how they expect lawyers to behave. Particularly at the start of a relationship, people tend to take each other at face value. You may have experienced this. If you look young for your age, clients may have doubted your expertise. Reversing those prejudices can have a powerful effect. A client who is expecting the lawyer to be overbearing or impatient will be charmed and very responsive when you come across as helpful and interested.

1.6 SUMMARY

Your ability to accept and use information empathetically and constructively will influence the professional relationship. The client who is consulting a lawyer needs to learn that the lawyer has a right to privileged or private information. The client who grasps this is better able to disclose all the facts. Whether this process happens quickly or slowly depends to a large extent on the lawyer's ability to create a good working and professional relationship.

When you realise that your client is not participating fully, it is sometimes difficult to identify why. In the past, lawyers have not been trained to think about the underlying conflicts which can act as blockages to communication. It is your task and responsibility to eliminate or reduce barriers to communication and to build bridges and use ways of behaving which improve interaction.

1.6.1 Checklist for creating the right climate

(a) Create the right physical and emotional climate.

(b) Empathise do not sympathise.

(c) Make the law accessible.

(d) Make the interview for the client, not you.

(e) Do not judge.

(f) Conform to expectations, not stereotypes.

(g) Know the client's business.

Chapter Two

Listening Skills

2.1 THE ACTIVE EAR

Although the predominant form of communication in interviews is questions asked by the lawyer, to be an effective interviewer you need to develop the skill of listening. Lawyers are often too busy asking questions to listen properly. Attentive listening involves showing the client that you have both heard and understood. Listening is an important aid to empathetic understanding and the client who feels listened to and heard will be encouraged to cooperate with the lawyer.

Professional listening is a skill which can be developed. It is an unusual person who can listen and concentrate for 100 per cent of the time. It is not enough merely to sit back and pay attention. To be a good listener requires:

(a) Concentration.

(b) Active participation.

(c) Watching for non-verbal signals.

(d) Taking account of feelings as well as the legal content.

(e) Practice.

2.2 BARRIERS TO LISTENING

A whole variety of factors can inhibit concentration and listening. If you are stressed, overworked, or anxious about a particular meeting, it will affect your ability to listen. If you are preoccupied with yourself or with the impression you are creating, this will affect your ability to concentrate on your client's concerns.

If the subject-matter is unusual, it is likely to attract attention; equally, if it is very familiar it will not. If we expect someone to be a boring speaker, that person may well fulfil our expectations and we may not listen carefully.

Physical factors can also inhibit the ability to listen. Apart from the obvious like a hearing disorder, if you are in poor health, feel drowsy or overworked, it will affect your concentration. The physical conditions of the room can also affect your ability to understand and hear what is being said. Poor acoustics or lighting, the wrong room temperature or extraneous noise can impair concentration.

Try to develop an awareness of your own blocks to listening and make a conscious effort not to put up blocks. It takes a lot of self-discipline to ignore someone else's poor speaking technique and to listen to the problem. It takes hard work to look interested and encouraging and not be distracted by noise or uncomfortable surroundings.

Selective listening is a problem for many people. It entails listening to what we think is important and filtering out the irrelevant. It is a dangerous trap for a lawyer because you might filter out something significant. If you do not train yourself to listen professionally, there is a danger that you may hear only what you want or expect to hear.

Another potential impediment is caused by the difference between speed of thought and talking speed. The average person speaks at about 125 words a minute, whereas most people think at approximately 500 words a minute. If you cannot slow down your thought processes to concentrate on the speaker, you will become distracted and your thoughts will wander.

Lack of interest in the content, or negative reactions to the speaker or the speaker's behaviour, can also affect concentration. If you find something offensive or distracting in a client's manner or tone of voice it can affect concentration.

Adopt attending behaviour. You show this by your body language. Non-verbal communication, or body language, is considered in chapter 6. If you feel your attention is wandering, alter your body posture occasionally to keep your attention from drifting. Try also writing down key words as a reminder. Show the client, by your behaviour, that you are listening. Note-taking is considered further in chapter 4.

There is more to listening than simply paying attention to what the client is saying. There are passive listening activities, which require minimal intervention by the lawyer, but which are very effective for encouraging clients to talk, and active listening, or paraphrasing, which entails summarising the essence of the client's words.

2.3   PASSIVE LISTENING

2.3.1   Silence

Silence is an important tool for the lawyer. Do not view it as merely the absence or opposite of speech. Clients need time to think and recollect. When you ask a question, allow time for the client to think before answering. Do not fill a pause immediately with another question. Try to develop the ability to cope with silences and use them to enhance communication. What may seem a long pause to you may not to the client who is thinking. If you have difficulty with pauses, consider counting silently to 10 before you ask another question.

Silence can be used constructively or destructively. Obviously this depends on how the client is behaving. If you think that the silence is a sign of sadness, distress or anger, long pauses will not necessarily be helpful. Switch then to asking questions to help the client talk.

2.3.2   Non-committal responses

If you feel that total silence is unnerving the client, use reinforcing expressions to acknowledge and encourage conversation. There are a variety of non-committal responses, ranging from encouraging noises like 'Umm', 'Ah' and 'Oh', which signify that you are paying attention, to head nods, encouraging looks and smiles. When you make non-committal noises, try to keep your tone of voice relatively neutral. 'Oh' can convey a range of emotions including surprise, excitement, boredom and disapproval, depending on the tone of voice used.

Encouraging facial expressions usually take the form of slightly raised eyebrows, an alert gaze, and may be accompanied by smiling. Smiling is generally interpreted as a friendly or supportive expression, but take care to smile only at appropriate moments. If you smile out of embarrassment or discomfort, it can be very off-putting.

2.3.3   Supportive statements

Supportive statements are the verbal equivalent of non-committal responses. Statements like 'I see', 'And then?', 'That's interesting, go on', all provide encouragement to a client to talk and show that you are listening.

2.3.4   Extension questions

Questions can be used as a prompt and also to reassure the client that you are concentrating. Avoid using simple interrogatives like 'Why?' and 'When?' which can sometimes be intrusive. Use instead an extension like 'And what happened next?' or, 'What did you do then?' or 'When did you leave?'

2.4   ACTIVE LISTENING

The passive listening techniques described above show the client that you are attending, but they are not particularly interactive. As well as using passive listening techniques, use paraphrasing, or active listening, to show the client that you have heard and understood what is being said. People sometimes find it difficult to say exactly what they mean, but they give clues, by the way they speak or in their choice of words. Active listening involves more than simply listening to words. It means listening for those clues.

Paraphrasing, or active listening, is a specific listening technique. The process involves taking account of what the client is saying, summarising it briefly and reflecting it back to the client. It is a powerful aid to empathetic communication. It is also an excellent listening tool for the professional relationship, but not something you would use consistently in everyday conversation.

The skill in paraphrasing lies not just in restating the words of the other person, but also restating or reflecting the meaning. Summarise what you have understood from the client's statements, in your own words. Generally it encourages the client to clarify and expand on the original statement. Paraphrasing not only helps you to understand, it also helps clients to clarify their thoughts. If you have paraphrased wrongly the client will soon correct you.

Example 1

> Client: 'I was absolutely furious when she walked out. How was I supposed to manage? Looking after the kids, working long hours, how could I take care of them properly?'
>
> Lawyer: 'So you were worried that you would not be able to manage your job and look after the children?'

Example 2

> Client: 'I built that company up from nothing over the past 10 years. I've sacrificed everything for it, some would say my marriage and family. And now, some large operation, which goes round preying on small businesses, wants to take over my company and turn it into yet another of its subsidiaries. Well, they have picked the wrong one this time. I'm not giving in without a fight.'
>
> Lawyer: 'Let's see if I understand you correctly. What you're saying is that your business means so much to you that you want to resist this takeover?'

As you are reflecting not simply the words, but also the feelings behind the words, you are listening on three levels:

(a)   To the actual words.

(b)   For the feelings behind the words. You will pick up clues from the pace of speech, choice of words, tone of voice and sentence structure. Clients may also specifically describe their feelings..

(c)   For intentions, to discover what the client is really trying to say or do.

The main active listening techniques are keyword repetition and the reflective statement.

Keyword repetition is very straightforward and involves simply repeating key phrases or words used by the client.

Example 1

Client: 'After he did that I decided that I would never speak to him again.'

Lawyer: 'Never?'

Example 2

Witness: 'I saw him. He used to shout at her – be really abusive, even threatening. And then one day I saw him hit her.'

Lawyer: 'He hit her?'

The reflective statement is the true active listening technique. It is a paraphrased summary showing that you empathise with and understand the client's feelings. It is characterised by introductory statements like 'So you felt that...?' or, 'So it seems to you that...?' Statements like 'As I understand it...?' or, 'If I've got it right...?' signal that you are summarising and inviting the client to confirm or contradict your summary.

2.5 SUMMARY

Listening to the client entails not simply listening for the facts but also for information on feelings about the problem. As a lawyer you may feel that your only concern is for the legal content of the client's problem. However, the client's feelings can tell you what action that client is hoping for or is likely to accept, how likely the client is to agree to a settlement or whether the client is proposing to fight.

Identifying and recognising a client's feelings is not the same as getting involved. Naturally as a lawyer you are primarily concerned with the legal issues, but the good lawyer will recognise that it is just as important to gather as much information as possible about the client's feelings.

Striking a good working relationship with your clients is important. It may demand a considerable degree of flexibility on your part. Being a good, professional listener is essential. This means being alert, attentive and concentrating. It entails employing a variety of passive and active listening techniques and addressing the client's feelings as well as the legal content of the problem.

2.5.1 Checklist: are you a good listener?

Do you:

(a)   Take the speaker seriously even when you do not find the content interesting?

(b)   Sit where you can see and hear the speaker?

(c)   Concentrate on the key points?

(d)   Look interested?

(e)   Ignore mannerisms, accents, dress etc?

(f)   Listen 'between the lines'?

(g)   Observe body language and feelings?

(h)   Think about what is being said?

(i)   Refrain from interrupting?

(j)   Allow for your own bias when evaluating?

(k)   Reflect back meaning not just words?

2.5.2   Checklist for good listening

(a)   Keep an open mind – do not be judgmental.

(b)   Assess the content not the delivery.

(c)   Listen for the main ideas.

(d)   Be flexible.

(e)   Prevent distractions.

(f)   Capitalise on thought speed – use any spare thinking time to concentrate on what is being said, not to allow your thoughts to wander.

(g)   Identify the feelings behind the content.

(h)   Listen and watch for non-verbal cues.

(i)   Mix passive and active listening techniques – nods and noises with verbal feedback.

(j)   Reflect back meaning not words.

(k)   Remember, silence is golden – use it constructively.

Chapter Three

Questioning Skills

3.1 GETTING TO THE HEART OF THE MATTER

The right question asked in the right way will yield good-quality
information. The wrong question will yield little or no information
at all. Often people ask questions without giving sufficient thought to
the kind of information they require. When you ask questions, you
should also be sensitive to a client's posture, facial reactions and
other non-verbal cues, since these are an additional source of
information. This chapter will explore different types of questions,
their limitations and how to construct a sequence of questions.
Non-verbal communication is considered later in chapter 6.

3.2 INFORMATION GATHERING

Your task, particularly in the first meeting, is to gather information
on the client's problem and views on possible solutions or action. You
must discover, sift for the relevant and analyse. Information
gathering is broader than fact-finding. It is also concerned with
discovering views, feelings and attitudes. When you are gathering and
reviewing information, distinguish between facts, inferences and
versions. Facts are (theoretically) objectively verifiable. An inference
is a conclusion which may or may not be correct. A 'version' is one
person's perspective of a state of affairs or set of events and may or

may not be correct. You need to distinguish between these and to avoid elevating versions or inferences to the status of facts.

Develop a variety of questioning styles for extracting information, to confirm your understanding of responses and to check for clarification. Recognising different types of questions, and their effect, makes it a lot easier to ask the right question. It will help you to think more clearly about what sort of information you hope to collect from each question. You are also asking questions to help clients recall past events. Memory tends to be selective. Unpleasant experiences or trauma can cloud memory. Sometimes people modify or distort past experiences because the reality does not fit with how they would like it to be. You will need to be alive to this possibility when you ask questions.

Part of the questioning process may entail you 'teaching' clients about what information you need. Often the cues lawyers give clients are very subtle. A client may gather that a particular question has been answered satisfactorily by an approving head nod from the lawyer or because a note was made of the answer. If a response was inadequate for the lawyer's purposes, it is likely to be followed by an additional or probing question. If the client digresses or provides irrelevant information, the lawyer discourages this behaviour by suggesting a return to the main topic. Gradually a pattern emerges as an interview progresses and clients learn what kind of information the lawyer wants. Generally this process is helpful, although you should take care that clients do not try to 'help' too much by selecting and telling you what they think you need to know. It is your task to do the editing and selection.

3.3 FORMULATING QUESTIONS

The quality of the relationship between you and your client depends to a large extent on the quality of your questions. Well-worded questions will help the communication process; unclear or clumsy questions may have the opposite effect. If clients do not see the relevance of questions, they may not give their full attention to answering. Suppose a client has come to see you because she suffered a back injury at work and she wishes to claim compensation. You are asking questions about what she does in her spare time. She may feel puzzled by this line of questioning, not necessarily say so, but become guarded in her responses. It is up to you to explain that her inability to enjoy activities which she did previously is taken into account when assessing her compensation.

When you introduce a new line of questioning, reiterate the general purpose of the interview and explain how that new line of questioning fits into the overall pattern. A client who fails to see the relevance of questions may give unsatisfactory answers. This process is particularly important when asking about a sensitive issue. Some topics are very difficult or embarrassing for clients to discuss. Being asked a question about a highly personal matter may cause a client to clam up, but it will be easier to get a response if the client understands why you need to know.

When formulating a question, word it so that the client understands the frame of reference. Even ordinary words like 'tall', 'short' or 'heavy' have different meanings to different people. If you are asking a client to describe someone's height, rather than say, 'Was he tall?', it is safer to ask, 'How tall was he?', giving some height indications as points of reference.

Similarly, a question such as 'How have you been managing since our last meeting?' could produce a range of answers. Do you want to know how the client has been managing emotionally, financially or in some other way? If it is the former, be more explicit and use words like 'financially' or 'for money' to prompt for the information you want. Phrase your questions so that clients understand their relevance.

One decision you will sometimes have to make is how you are going to ask for information, particularly on potentially sensitive matters. Sometimes a direct question will be appropriate, whereas on other occasions a series of general questions, which circle the problem, will be the better approach. There are no hard-and-fast rules. What you decide will depend on the type of interview, the circumstances, for example, whether this is the first meeting, the type of legal problem involved and how well you know the client.

3.4 TYPES OF QUESTION

Questions are generally classified in terms of the breadth of information they aim to extract. Different types of question produce very different answers. As a general principle, keep an open mind in the early stages of the interview or meeting and ask broad, or open questions. Try not to narrow the scope of your enquiries until you are sure you have obtained a broad picture of the problem.

3.4.1 Open questions

Open questions simply establish the topic and leave the client free to select either the subject-matter for discussion or the information which the client believes to be relevant.

Lawyer: 'How can I help?'

Lawyer: 'Perhaps you could tell me why you have come to see me today?'

Open questions are particularly useful in the early stages of an interview for creating the right climate for discussion. If you think back to your own experiences of interviews, you will probably recollect that there were often some warm-up questions about the weather, the journey or finding the venue. These are called *contact* questions and are simply a form of open question. They are not really asked to gather information, but to establish rapport and to give the client something easy and neutral to talk about.

One of the attractions of open questions is that the client can select what answer to give. Even if the information you receive is not automatically what you consider to be relevant, the client's choice of subject-matter is highly significant and should give you some clues about concerns and expectations.

Asking clients open questions gives them a freedom which carries with it certain responsibilities on your part. It is important that you do not interrupt the answer. If you are in a hurry to get to the point, or unable for some reason to listen attentively, you could damage the relationship by inviting the client to talk and then showing either directly, or non-verbally, that you are not interested. You will be sending mixed messages. Do not ask open questions if you cannot train yourself to be an attentive listener. Answers to open questions yield the most information of all, but only if you are really listening and attending. As well as the content, the client's tone of voice, use of pauses, phrasing and non-verbal communication give information.

Clients who like to talk or who cannot stick to the point may see the open question as a green light to ramble. It is still worth asking open questions but if you know your client has a tendency to ramble, try prefacing the question with something like, 'briefly' or 'in a few words'. If you really feel that time is slipping away from you or that you are losing control of the interview, you can then change to a different style of questioning.

Very occasionally a client may feel inhibited by being invited to talk in an unstructured way. Open questions can be too broad where a problem is highly personal. Provided you are listening and watching closely, you should be able to spot this. If you see the client is in difficulty, try using a series of narrow questions to gather information.

Allow time at the end of the meeting for more open questions and use them to perform a kind of sweeping-up function. Ask questions like 'Is there anything else that you think might be relevant?' or 'Is there anything else troubling you?' By broadening out your enquiries at the end of the meeting you can double-check that you have not missed any vital information.

3.4.2   Probe questions

As the name implies, this type of question is designed to dig for information and to get beyond potentially superficial replies. The best type of probe question draws on active listening techniques and does not make the client feel interrogated. Probe questions are useful for clarifying statements, discovering a client's feelings about a problem or events and checking for understanding. However, if used too early, probe questions may act as inhibitors.

Since lawyers are often pressed for time, they tend to fall into the habit of using probe and closed questions as an efficient way of extracting and developing information. As a style of questioning it is useful, but only as part of a portfolio of questioning techniques.

Probe to encourage clients to expand on topics. Simple *interrogative* questions like, 'Why?', 'How long?' and 'When?' are all obvious examples of probe questions. You can ask a question in this rather terse form, but consider softening it by adding a few follow-up words:

'Why do you say that?' instead of 'Why?'

'At what time of day did this happen?' instead of 'When?'

Longer interrogatives like this are sometimes called *extension* questions.

Other ways of probing are in fact variants on active listening techniques. *Keyword repetition* is one. You simply pick up what you think is the message or key idea from the client's words and repeat it, using an interrogative tone of voice. It indicates that you think a phrase is important and that you would like to hear more.

Client: 'We had a lot of aggravation from the landlord of the premises because there was a forfeiture clause in the lease. As we were subtenants of the tenants, when they went into liquidation, we were kicked out.'

Lawyer: 'You say there was a forfeiture clause?'

A modified form of keyword repetition is the *mirror* or *reverse question*. As the name suggests, the lawyer uses reflection, in this case a statement made by the client. Once again, the tone of voice suggests that more development is required.

Client: 'I thought about preparing a plan'.

Lawyer: 'You thought you would make a plan?'

Keyword repetition and mirror questions work well with clients who are able or keen to talk, but a client who does not wish to expand on a statement can easily sidestep fairly gentle probing with a simple affirmative. Consequently, whereas the previous mirror question might have been taken by the client as a cue to describe what kind of plan he had in mind, it might equally have been answered with a simple 'Yes'. An alternative question here for the lawyer is 'What was your plan?' This is more direct and could be used where you are concerned that the client might sidestep the other question.

Reflective questions are useful for summarising and testing with the client what you understand the client's feelings or problem to be. The reflective question paraphrases what the client has said and invites clarification.

> Client: 'At the beginning of July, I saw John Wright, the group's chief executive. He told me that he was moving us to offices in Slough in two weeks' time. That was the only notice I had – just two weeks to get things organised.'
>
> Lawyer: 'Did you feel that you should have been given more notice?'

Prefacing your question with words like 'So it seems to you that . . .?', or 'You feel that . . .?', followed by your understanding of the problem, will give the client an opportunity to agree or disagree with your evaluation.

You can use active and passive listening techniques in a number of ways when probing for more information. Supportive statements like 'That's interesting', 'Go on' and 'So how did you feel then?' all show the client that you are listening and wish to hear more. Brief assenting comments like 'I see' and simple encouraging requests for more information like 'Tell me about it', even well-timed pauses, will all encourage clients to talk. 'I should like to hear more' is a direct bid for information but is not as aggressive as 'What do you mean?'

Similarly, a *summary* question, which concentrates on factual content, is a useful mechanism for confirming understanding. Sometimes called a *confirming* or *crystallising* question, the summary question briefly reviews the facts and invites clarification. The

summary is generally preceded by statements like 'As I understand it
. . .?' or 'So what you are saying is . . .?' This type of question is a
useful follow-up to open questions. When the client has described the
problem, you can then recap.

The summary question is also a useful device for controlling a client
who cannot stick to the point or who takes a long time to explain.
One tactic is, of course, to interrupt. If you are really desperate, a
statement like 'If we could just return to the question' is effective, but
some clients may find it very off-putting. Thanking the client and then
indicating in a more subtle way that you would like the answers to
keep to the point may be just as effective.

> Lawyer: 'Thank you. That was interesting and we may need to
> come back to that. Now time is running a little short so I wonder
> if you could summarise for me what happened next. I'd like to get
> an idea of the broad picture before we examine some of the details.'

If you are trying to gather more information from the client, a
comparative question is useful for making an evaluation on a before-
and-after basis.

> Lawyer: 'What was the situation like between you and your
> husband before you moved?'

> Client: 'Well, it wasn't ideal but at least . . .'

> Lawyer: 'And how did things change after you moved house?'

Hypothetical questions are sometimes useful to encourage the client
to express a view on possible courses of action and solutions.
Hypotheticals are generally signified by 'What if' statements of one
kind or another. They are a useful device for testing views and
feelings, provided the example you pose is one with which the client
can identify.

> Lawyer: 'How would you feel if . . .?'

> 'What would your response be if . . .?'

Try to avoid using a *multiple* question, in other words, a question which contains more than one question in the same sentence. For example:

> Lawyer: 'Do you feel that the bank should have warned you before they contacted the creditors or were you expecting something like that to happen anyway?'

The real danger of the multiple question is that it can lead to misunderstandings. In the previous example the answer given by the client to one of the two questions might be interpreted by the lawyer as applying to the other question.

3.4.3 Narrow or closed questions

Narrow questions are a kind of probe. They select and confine the subject-matter and determine the breadth of the response. This type of question is used to elicit specific items of information. It requires comparatively little effort from the client to respond and correspondingly more effort from the lawyer, who is taking control by defining the question and indicating possible answers:

> Lawyer: 'At what time did the accident happen?'

> 'How long have you and your husband been married?'

One possible danger of asking narrow questions, particularly early on in the relationship, is that they may inhibit rapport. Some clients feel at a disadvantage in the unfamiliar territory of a solicitor's office. They may even be feeling at a disadvantage by having to admit to a problem. If you start the interview by asking a series of narrow questions, you immediately put the client into a passive mode. Clients take their cue from their lawyers on how to behave and on what sort of responses are expected. If you principally ask narrow questions, your clients may soon believe that all you expect are answers to specific questions and that if you do not ask about a topic it cannot be important. Creating that kind of attitude in your clients could prevent them from volunteering crucial information.

Many fact-finding questions start with simple interrogatives like 'Who?', 'What?', 'When?' and 'Where?' These were discussed in 3.4.2; they are sometimes also called *identification* questions because they are asked to identify something specific like a place, a time or a person. Some lawyers get straight into this style of questioning, asking clients for names, addresses, dates of birth and other standard information. It is easy for clients to answer these questions and it can be argued that it helps to settle clients down.

Consider whether this information could be provided by the client completing a form before the interview, which you then go through with the client when you meet, or whether the details could be taken by a receptionist, secretary or paralegal. Alternatively, wait until you have some idea from the client of what the problem is before you start asking for standard information.

Narrow questions are particularly useful for reiterating, clarifying detail and checking facts. If a topic is sensitive, a series of narrow questions might enable the client to talk more freely than when responding to an open question. However, they are potentially dangerous in that they can encourage the client to be passive.

3.4.4   Leading and yes/no questions

The structure of a leading question is such that it provides the information which the lawyer believes is relevant and encourages the client simply to confirm a proposition. Many leading questions require simple yes/no answers. They are all variations of the closed or narrow question:

> Lawyer: 'You had been drinking that evening, had you not?'

> 'You were not surprised, then, when you were asked to leave at once?'

It is dangerous to prompt an answer, particularly at an early stage of the interview. Apart from possibly inhibiting rapport, some clients may be tempted to agree with a statement, even if it is not correct. Clients may want to please their lawyers or at least present themselves favourably. Giving an affirmative nod to a leading question is often easier for a client than disagreeing with a statement. A client who has something to conceal may find evasion easier when asked only closed questions.

Nevertheless, questions phrased for a closed response do have their uses, particularly for checking or confirming information. You can also use leading questions to lead a client through sensitive or delicate issues, by asking a series of leading questions.

3.5   CREATING A SEQUENCE OF QUESTIONS

Some people liken the questioning process to a funnel. The wide mouth of the funnel represents the early stages of an interview where open questions are asked in order to gather as much information as possible. As you progress through the interview, narrow and probe questions are asked to check and clarify the information. These

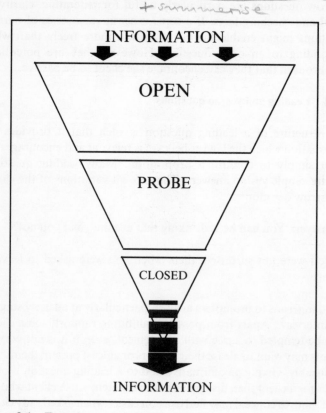

Figure 3.1   Funnel

represent the narrow neck of the funnel. The idea is that when the story and the problem emerge at the end of the funnel, they have been filtered by questions and the information is refined and relevant. In this model, open questions are asked to draw in as much information as possible and the refining process is achieved by probe and closed questions (see figure 3.1).

Other commentators have described this sequence as a 'T-bar', with the horizontal bar representing the open question stage and the vertical representing the clarification and summary stage (see figure 3.2). Both models are essentially the same since the earlier stages of the interview are regarded as the right time to trawl for information.

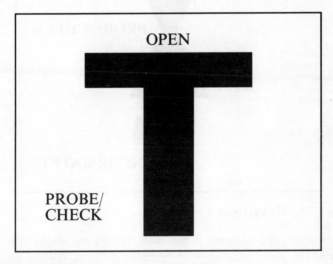

Figure 3.2   T-bar

Organising your questions into a sequence according to either of these models is useful. It will encourage you to do some advance planning, to think about the different possible ways of gathering information and the impact that questioning has on clients. The funnel and T-bar approaches encourage you to view all information as being potentially useful.

There is always a danger, in any interview or meeting, that vital information is not collected. It may therefore be better, if you wish to visualise a sequence, to view it as an X or hourglass (see figure 3.3). This sequence or model has a wide opening at either end, but narrows in the middle. If you follow this model, you will be checking and clarifying information in the middle of your meeting.

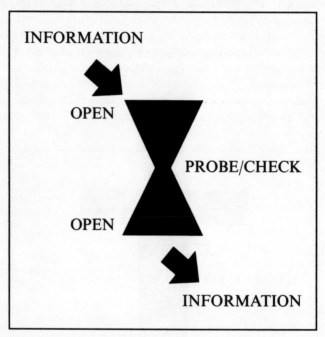

Figure 3.3   Hourglass or X

Representing the sequence in this way encourages you to open up your line of questioning towards the end of the interview and to do a final trawl for information. It is not always easy for clients to recall facts and details. Some clients may have come prepared but you will be using questions to jog the memories of those who have not.

Trawling for information in the later stages of the interview is a wise precaution and may prevent some nasty surprises later.

Lawyer: 'Is there anything else you think I need to know?'

'Is there anyone else who might have an interest in this, whom you haven't previously mentioned?'

Another form of sequence is the 'inverted' funnel where you start with closed questions and gradually broaden out to open questions (see figure 3.4). This model is not recommended unless you already have a good relationship with the client. However, it is a useful approach if you have very little time available, if your client has a tendency to ramble, or where the subject-matter is so sensitive or difficult that the client needs to be led through it. If you propose to follow this model, ensure that you have first established a good rapport with your client.

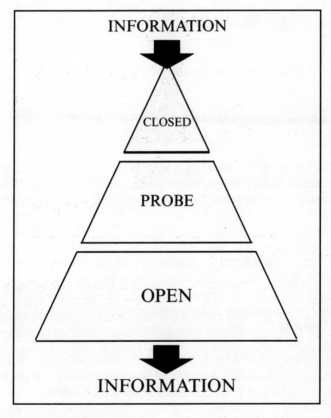

Figure 3.4   Inverted funnel

3.6   CLIENT RELUCTANCE

There are many reasons why clients give inadequate responses to questions. They may genuinely not understand the question, either because of the language you have used or the concepts. They may not have enough knowledge to answer the question in the depth you require. Perhaps the client cannot remember or possibly the question was too intrusive. If an answer is not what you expected or needed, try to avoid any hint of implied criticism when you probe further. Use the second of the two following approaches:

Lawyer: 'Well, that wasn't what I was asking you. What I said was . . .'

'I understand. And how about . . .?'

3.7   QUESTIONING WITNESSES WHEN PREPARING FOR TRIAL

The techniques for questioning a witness are substantially the same as for clients. Follow the standard process of establishing rapport and explaining the purpose and format of the interview. Witnesses are no different from clients in that they too need to be encouraged to communicate fully. In fact you may have to work even harder to encourage a witness to talk. Witnesses are often meeting lawyers to help with someone else's problem, rather than their own, and therefore derive little benefit from getting involved. Consequently some witnesses are very reluctant to meet the client's lawyer. Bear it in mind as a possibility and reassure witnesses of the value of their contributions.

If a witness shows reluctance, you could try encouraging involvement by suggesting that a full statement at this stage might avoid the later need for legal proceedings. There is a slight danger, however, that this approach could backfire. You are playing on the witness's fear of going to court to try to encourage cooperation. Raising the spectre of going to court could make the witness even more reluctant to become involved. If that is so you will have to reassure the witness about appearing in court. Explain how the case will be conducted, when the witness is likely to be called and what he or she can expect. Appeals to the witness's importance in the scheme of things, and the value of the testimony may act as encouragement, particularly to people who are public spirited.

There are differing views on how to structure a sequence of questions for a witness interview. One view is that you should always start with open questions. Once you feel that you have gathered all the potentially relevant information, use a variety of probe and closed questions to verify and clarify the material and its relevance to the client matter. This is the standard funnel or T-bar approach.

Another school of thought would have you follow the inverted funnel model. Since the main purpose of the interview is to check the story for corroboration and consistency, closed and probe questions can set the right tone for the meeting. If you intend to follow the inverted funnel approach, allow for open questions at the end of the meeting to ensure that you have swept up all possible loose ends. In other words, rather than the simple inverted funnel, use in preference the X model.

Quite a lot of preparation needs to be done before interviewing a witness. Unlike a normal client interview which you approach with an open mind, lawyers question witnesses because they are checking a story, looking for discrepancies or contradictions and preparing a case. Often there is a dispute between opposing parties about the facts. The lawyer is looking for information which doubts and discredits the opposition's version.

You may want to use the meeting to evaluate your witness's ability to appear sound and to cope in court with questions and under pressure. Some lawyers adopt a slightly hectoring or aggressive approach when questioning witnesses to assess how well that person will stand up to cross-examination. This can, after all, have a bearing on whether you call that witness. If you adopt this approach, explain what you are about to do and why. It should prevent any bad feeling arising. Lawyers tend not to explain, perhaps fearing that they will lose the element of surprise. In fact, explaining what you are about to do is courteous and will still enable you to 'test' your witness.

3.8   SUMMARY

Try to frame questions in language which your clients will understand
and introduce questions in a way which permits clients to see their
relevance. Use a variety of questioning techniques. Try to start with
open questions. Listen closely to the answers as these may well give
you clues on what to ask next. As the discussion continues, use a
mixture of reflective questions, repeating the content for clarification,
and closed questions, defining the potential answers, to establish facts
and check back information.

Try to avoid using 'Why?' and 'What?' too often in case it makes you
seem aggressive. Follow-up questions like, 'What was it you heard?'
and general probes such as 'Anything else?' will show that you are
listening and will encourage the client to talk. Do not be afraid to give
the client pauses and silence to reflect and recall. Limit your use of
leading questions and try to keep your questions short. Concentrate
on one idea at a time. If you ask multiple or complicated questions,
you run the risk of confusing some clients and irritating others.

Be flexible in your approach. You can, and should, plan in advance
and work to a possible structure and sequence of questions.
Obviously a structure is just a guide to be tried, modified and
sometimes abandoned. You can work out your own model. The
overriding concerns are creating the right climate for the client to give
you the information you require and being flexible in order to meet
the needs of your client.

3.8.1   Checklist for asking questions

(a)   Ask straightforward uncomplicated questions.

(b)   Use language the client will understand.

(c)   Vary your questioning style; use a mixture of open, closed and
probe questions.

(d)   Make questions relevant to the client's concerns.

(e)   Work out a structure and sequence for your interviews and
meetings and consider using checklists.

(f)   Use passive and active listening techniques to support your use of questions.

3.8.2   Glossary of types of question

Closed to gather, develop and clarify information (see 3.4.3).

Comparative to encourage assessments or evaluation, for variety (see 3.4.2).

Confirming see summary in 3.8.

Contact to establish rapport (see 3.4.1).

Crystallising see summary in 3.8.

Extension to encourage development of statements (see 3.4.2).

Hypothetical to encourage expression of views on solutions and course of action (see 3.4.2).

Identification to extract specific items of information (see 3.4.3).

Interrogative to encourage development (see 3.4.2).

Leading for checking and confirmation (see 3.4.4).

Mirror a variation of active listening, to encourage development (see 3.4.2).

Multiple to be avoided at all costs (see 3.4.2).

Narrow see Closed.

Open to establish rapport, to 'trawl' for information (see 3.4.1).

Probe for clarification, developing information, checking detail (see 3.4.2).

Reflective for summarising, for testing understanding (see 3.4.2).

Repetition (keyword) a form of active listening, to test for understanding (see 3.4.2).

Reverse see Mirror.

Summary to confirm understanding, to recap, to direct and control the interview (see 3.4.2).

Yes/no see Leading.

Chapter Four

Managing the Interview

4.1 FOCUSING YOURSELF TO FOCUS THE CLIENT

There is more to an interview than simply establishing a favourable pattern of communication. If you do not have a clear idea of what you hope to achieve, the interview could turn into a rambling and unstructured exchange. Preparation and a clear sense of objectives will help you plan and structure your meeting.

4.2 PREPARATION

4.2.1 Preparing yourself

Even if this is your first meeting with the client you can still do some initial planning and preparation. Identify your objectives. They are likely to include:

(a) Establishing a good relationship with the client.

(b) Gathering sufficient information to enable you to make a preliminary diagnosis or explanation.

(c) Giving the client an outline of the legal position.

(d)   Finding out the client's expectations and intentions.

(e)   Explaining your firm's fee structure and discussing payment of fees.

When preparing for a meeting, what do you know about its purpose? Are there any files you can read beforehand? Are there any preliminary questions you can devise?

With new commercial clients, what can you find out about their companies in the financial or commercial press?

Do you have interview checklists to work from to help you organise the meeting?

If you are meeting an established client, what can you find out from a quick inspection of the files? Have matters been proceeding smoothly? Is the client likely to be seeing you about a continuation of a matter or for something new? If the meeting is one of a series, make sure that the file is current and that you have done everything you agreed to do at the last meeting.

Even if you cannot predict in advance precisely what the client wishes to discuss, you should try to do some preparation. Train the staff who book appointments and meetings to ask the client what the meeting is about. If a matter is referred to you from a partner or fee-earner, make time for a briefing.

4.2.2   Preparing the client

If you want to work effectively with clients, try to develop the kind of relationship where both of you take responsibility for information and matters within your respective spheres. Although some clients may want to off-load problems on to their lawyers, the majority would prefer to play some part in the management of their affairs.

Clients can be asked to bring to the meeting relevant documents, photographs or sketch maps. Apart from showing that you are taking the meeting seriously, you are involving the client in the process. Being asked to prepare helps the client to focus attention on the meeting and may assist recall of events. Information can always be produced later if the client forgets to bring it, but clients who come well prepared will gain more benefit. If the meeting is set for several days ahead, consider sending a short letter, confirming the date and time and asking the client to bring in any documentation.

4.3 TIMING

What is the best time of day to hold meetings and interviews? The answer is, of course, the best time for your clients, but it is not always possible to organise things so neatly. If you spend most of your mornings in court, then clearly interviews and meetings with clients will have to be held in the afternoon, evenings or even weekends. If you do have a choice, what are your working patterns and times of day when you perform best? Arrange meetings, if possible, for those times rather than at times when you find it difficult to concentrate.

Most solicitors are under a tremendous amount of pressure to process work in as short a time as possible. This sometimes means that they do not plan their time as effectively as they might. When you are arranging meetings and interviews, try to estimate realistically the time needed for each meeting. Build into each appointment a further 10–15 minutes for basic follow-up administrative work like dictating file notes and diarising dates. It is much easier to do this kind of follow-up activity when the information is still fresh. Other, significant follow-up activity will also have to be organised and planned into your work schedule.

4.4 THE ENVIRONMENT

Some firms use special rooms for meeting and interviewing clients. There is a lot to be said for this practice. Using special-purpose rooms makes it easier to reduce distractions and helps both parties to concentrate. If this is not the practice in your firm and you see clients in your office, keep it neat and tidy. If it looks a mess, clients might find it off-putting. You may think it gives an impression of activity and importance but clients may worry that you are too busy to handle their cases promptly. You will appear overworked rather than hardworking.

4.4.1   Seating

When you are considering the surroundings for a client meeting,
think about the seating arrangements and furniture. If you sit behind
a desk with the client opposite, this will not automatically lead to an
easy conversation. Some clients may expect you to sit behind a desk
and you may find it easier and more comfortable to sit there, where
you can see the client easily. It is, however, the standard position used
for confrontations, when people want to 'eyeball' each other. Your
manner can compensate for this but consider using other seating
arrangements.

One option is to sit to one side of the desk, at a 45 degree angle to
your client. You can then lean on the desk to take notes without
hiding or disappearing behind it. The angle at which you sit or stand
does have an impact on communication. Sitting side-by-side indicates cooperation or at least neutrality. Unfortunately it is not the
best position for observing the client when asking questions. Another
option is to start the interview sitting side-by-side, or at least at a 45
degree angle. When you have established eye contact and the right
climate, you can then move to a face-to-face position.

4.5   NOTE-TAKING

You will need an accurate record of what was said and agreed at all
your meetings, yet it can be difficult to take notes and give the client
your full attention. Looking down to take notes means that you can
lose eye contact and miss the client's non-verbal clues and signals.

You cannot hope to write down everything the client says. You will
find it impossible to keep the interview within reasonable time-limits.
The less experienced or confident you feel, the stronger will be the
urge to write everything down. Afterwards you will be faced with a
welter of information to digest and précis. If you have not read the
file, or you are not familiar with the matter, it is difficult to make
instant decisions about what to note. This is another reason why
preparation before the meeting is so important. People generally
cover themselves by noting everything, in the hope of making sense
of it later. As a trainee solicitor that may have been possible, although

it was inefficient. As a fee-earner with a full case-load, it is out of the question. You will be too busy and so you may have to rethink your method of note-taking.

There is no single, perfect way of taking notes and what suits one lawyer will not necessarily suit another. Equally, do not assume that what worked for you as a student at college will automatically translate to client meetings. For interviews in particular, try to develop a style which helps you to follow the thread of the client's story, to identify and note the key and subsidiary points, and maintain a good atmosphere.

Some clients will expect you to take notes; others may not have thought about it but will automatically accept it. Some clients will feel uncomfortable and will wonder what you are writing and where that information will end up. When you meet a client for the first time, explain that you propose to take notes as an *aide-mémoire*. You could offer to send a copy of the notes to the client as a record of what was discussed and agreed. That way the client will be kept informed and reassured that you have no secret purpose.

Your note-taking will not be constant in the interview. There will be points when you will need to take notes and others where you should listen and not record. As the client describes the problem or gives you an update on events, simply note down key points. As you clarify facts and events, expand your notes. Some lawyers prefer to take no notes at all, until they have reached a point in the interview where they feel they have a broad understanding of the problem.

As you take notes, you will be noting some points and not others. By doing this you could be unintentionally signalling to the client that some things are more important than others. Your client may then take a cue from you and edit some replies and amplify others. This can distort the story, so it is important to use a system which allows you to note briefly the essential and amplifying points.

Try to avoid taking very full notes in the early stages of the interview. Many solicitors get caught up too early on with collecting relatively basic information. They bombard clients with questions about dates of birth, addresses, marital status and so on. It can be argued that going through this sort of information with clients is a way of settling them down, but the information is generally too important and useful to be scribbled down hastily in the first few minutes. It is far better at the start to concentrate on creating the right atmosphere and discovering the problem.

The purpose of note-taking is to record facts, to aid recall and to help you plan action. Aim to develop a system of key points, with a clear, legible layout and a structured sequence of subheadings. Use symbols and abbreviations if these help, provided you (and your secretary) remember what they stand for. Use wide margins. Space the points out across the page. Apart from making your notes easier to read later, it will make it easier to add in extra information. Use indentations for subsidiary points.

Consider using prepared formats. One method is the outline or two-column layout, where main points are noted on the left-hand side of the page, and supporting details are noted on the right. Another suggestion, when you are taking instructions, is to work from standard checklists. If you know in advance what type of transaction the client wishes to discuss, working from a checklist will help you structure the interview and take notes. There is an example of a checklist at the end of this chapter as a model for developing your own.

If the client mentions something unusual, note down the phrasing exactly in the client's own words. Even if you have not fully understood, if you need to return to that point, you will find it easier to remind the client if you can use the same phrasing. It is also a good idea to ask the client to confirm the spelling of names, places or technical terms. As you note key points, repeat them to the client. The process of repetition can help concentration and recall.

Write up your notes as soon as possible after the interview. Allow time between appointments and train yourself to do it promptly. It does require self-discipline, particularly after a difficult interview, but it is a good practice to adopt. Your firm may have a policy on whether notes should be dictated and typed up or whether the manuscript notes (provided they are clean and legible) can be put straight on to the file. If not, make a commercial assessment. There is little point dictating, for typing up, a comparatively short, clear file note. On the other hand, lengthy notes of a meeting with counsel which may be read by a number of people should be typed.

4.5.1 Tape-recording interviews

If you want to record a face-to-face or telephone interview, it is sensible and polite to obtain the consent of the other party. Recording can be a useful adjunct to personal notes. However, you may still need a précis of the transcript, so you could end up listening to the interview twice. Having a transcript of the interview is an excellent back-up but it is no substitute for taking good notes at the interview.

4.6 STRUCTURING THE INTERVIEW

Chapter 3 explores how to structure an interview or meeting. In a first meeting or interview, when you are taking instructions, there will be many more things to explain to the client. Apart from finding out what is worrying the client, explaining the legal position and exploring solutions, there are business matters to cover. Fees, costs and billing procedures may need to be explored or explained.

Clearly, if you have dealt with a client before you will not have to discuss fees, unless your rates have changed, although it is still wise to do so to give the client a clear picture. If this is the first meeting, the client may also want an estimate of the likely cost of the legal work and how long the matter will take to resolve. Often this is difficult to predict, which is sometimes used as a reason for not giving this type of information. Even if the overall time-scale is in doubt, try to predict how long it will take to get to the next stage in the process. Explain what factors can affect progress and undertake to keep the client regularly informed of progress. Similarly, give some cost parameters.

There are a number of phases or stages to the interview:

    (a)   preliminary

(b)   description of the problem

(c)   clarification

(d)   advice

(e)   close.

4.6.1   Preliminary

It is your responsibility to put clients at ease. Offer refreshments and be as welcoming as possible. Animate your face, shake hands, use your clients' names and look pleased to see them. If other things are worrying you, put them out of your mind and concentrate on your client.

Explain how the interview will be conducted. You may need to explain how long you expect it to last, what format you propose to follow and what information you will be looking for. The length of your explanation will depend on the experience of the client. If this is the client's first visit to a lawyer, you will have to do more explaining. The client may have some preconceptions or expectations and a vague idea of what to expect. Some clients will be feeling apprehensive. They may feel that visiting their lawyer is like going to the dentist. Your task at this stage is to settle clients down and put them at ease.

The early stages of the interview are critical. It is up to you to make it relevant to the client's needs and goals. The reassurance you provide about confidentiality, and the ways in which you handle any resistance or reluctance to providing information, will set the tone for the whole relationship. Ask open questions to create the right climate for discussion.

4.6.2   Description of the problem

During the preliminary stage you may have done quite a lot of talking. It is important that you now let the client do the talking. Ask open questions to encourage the client to describe the problem or to update you on progress since the last meeting. Do not take notes until you have a good understanding of the issues. Use active and passive listening techniques to encourage the client to talk.

4.6.3 Clarification

Once you think that you have an understanding of the problem, you can then ask probe questions to clarify and to search for more detail. Reflective statements and active listening are also worth using to test your understanding with the client. Paraphrase and summarise the client's description of the problem or issues. Invite the client to confirm or correct your understanding. It is essential that you get it right. Try to restrict your use of leading questions to checking on very basic information.

4.6.4 Advice

If you are in a position to give an immediate diagnosis, do so. Clients like to know as soon as possible what their position is and what are their options. However, it can happen that you are not in a position to give a definitive answer there and then. If that is the case, tell the client when you will come back with the answer. Fix a deadline and stick to it. It is much better, if you are not sure, to check and give the right answer, rather than one which is only half right, or even possibly wrong. If you cannot say precisely what are the options or best courses of action, you should at least try to give an explanation of the issues, in non-technical language.

Your advice should, to a large extent, turn on the client's plans or wishes. You must help the client reach a decision by identifying the advantages and disadvantages in each possible choice. It is the client who makes the final decision but you can help by structuring the decision-making and evaluating the options.

Sometimes clients have already reached decisions about what they want to happen. If you feel that the client's ideas are wrong you should say so, giving your reasons. But is that enough? Should you try to persuade a client to change a decision? Provided no unfair pressure is applied, you can argue against a decision. Use active listening techniques to show you understand, before offering alternative solutions. Clients are more likely to listen to your alternative proposals if you first show that you understand why they have chosen particular options.

4.6.5   Closing the interview

Never close an interview or meeting without giving the client:

(a)   Some indication of what is expected to happen next.

(b)   An idea of the expected time-scale, i.e., when you will be active, when you expect to hear from the other side.

(c)   An update on fees (unless this is inappropriate, for example, in emergency injunction proceedings or if the client is fully legally aided).

(d)   An opportunity to consider whether any other information may be relevant.

It is particularly important that you allow time at the end of the meeting or interview to ask open questions to check for any additional relevant information. Give the client an opportunity also to ask you questions. Make sure that when you invite questions, you have adopted an open body posture which matches the invitation to question. Palms down, insufficient eye contact, putting your papers away, will all be signals to the client that you are not really serious about inviting questions. Keep track of the time in the interview so that there is always time for the client to bring up any additional matters or to ask you questions.

4.7   TELEPHONE INTERVIEWING

When you interview someone over the telephone, because you cannot see each other, you will have to work harder to establish and maintain good communication. You rely more heavily on verbal cues. Problems can occur in telephone interviews, particularly if you lack confidence. When you cannot see someone, you may imagine that person to be more knowledgeable, confident and in control. This puts you at a disadvantage. Having built up this picture, if you are unconfident, your voice may give you away. As your voice is your main asset, you are directly harming yourself.

Actively use your voice to create an aura of efficiency and self-confidence. Vary the pitch, tone, speed and emphasis. Speak slowly and clearly and try to sound positive, friendly and courteous. If you appear bored, distracted or unresponsive, the other party will take the lead from you and respond accordingly. If you are interviewing or speaking on the telephone, all the client hears is your tone of voice and any listening noises you make, which show that you are paying attention. Anger or irritation are easily detected. Because there is no visual contact, misunderstandings are more likely to occur than in a face-to-face meeting, so you must take care to create the right impression.

Before you telephone a client make sure that you are properly prepared. Read the file and the latest correspondence before you call. Make a list of the points you wish to make. If the client calls you and you are not ready to take the call, either ask the client to hold, while you get the file, or offer to call the client back shortly, when you are properly prepared.

Otherwise, the guidelines for conducting an interview over the telephone are the same as for a face-to-face interview. Ask open questions and make notes of the key points. At various stages, summarise and check back your understanding of details. Frequent use of summaries take the place of the normal nods and smiles which occur in face-to-face encounters. If the client is incoherent or is having difficulty explaining, you may need to switch to closed and probe questions to give direction.

If a client is upset or angry, you will need to diffuse that tension. Listen sympathetically and try to remain objective. Allow the client to let off steam. Ask open questions to get to the bottom of the complaint and keep asking questions until you are quite sure you understand the problem. Work out a solution with the client. Even if the problem is not caused by you or your office, try to help the client in some way. Would making a call on the client's behalf ease or solve the problem? If so, offer to do it. Whenever you end a telephone call, do so positively, leaving both of you in no doubt about what the next step will be, and if you agree to do something, make sure you do it.

Perhaps it is obvious, but do familiarise yourself with all the facilities of your telephone. Know how to divert and transfer a call without cutting off the caller. Do not carry on two conversations at once, one with the caller and one with someone in your room. If you have to say something which you do not want a client to hear, put the client briefly on hold, explaining what you are doing. Do not put your hand over the mouthpiece because the client may still be able to hear. If you are proposing to use your telephone's loudspeaker or tape-recording facilities, explain this in advance to the client and confirm that it is acceptable.

4.8   SUMMARY

It is your responsibility to manage the interview, to create the right conditions for the exchange of information and to keep accurate records of what is discussed. As with so many things, preparation is essential. Schedule your working day so that you allow time to prepare yourself and the physical environment. Encourage your clients to come prepared to meetings. This will be easier with commercial clients, but most people cooperate when they understand why they are asked to do something.

Telephone interviewing is as important as face-to-face interviewing and requires the same amount of preparation.

Note-taking is always difficult, whatever the forum, so consider developing checklists or some other format to assist you. The more adept you become at taking clean, accurate notes in an unobtrusive fashion, the better equipped you will be at managing the interview process and progressing it through its various stages.

4.8.1   Checklist for taking instructions

Client details

   (a)   Surname/last name:

   (b)   First name(s):

   (c)   Home address:

       Tel:

   (d)   Occupation:

   (e)   Next of kin:

       Address:

   (f)   How client came to consult: referral, through advertising, recommendation, other

   (g)   Legal aid: yes/no

   (h)   Payment on account: yes/no

Matter details

   (a)   Nature of matter: personal injury claim – road traffic accident

   (b)   Other party(ies)

       1   Name and address:

       2   Name and address:

       3   Name and address:

   (c)   Name and address of insurers:

   (d)   Name and address of other party's(ies') insurers:

   (e)   Client's doctor:

       Name and address:

   (f)   Description of injury(ies):

(g)   Description of how injury occurred:

(h)   Police report: yes/no

(i)   Weather report: yes/no

(j)   Expert medical evidence required: yes/no

(k)   Any other expert's report required: yes/no

4.8.2   Checklist for interview management

(a)   Give the client a warm welcome.

(b)   Adopt an open body posture.

(c)   Emphasise confidentiality.

(d)   Ask open questions to discover the problem.

(e)   Use passive and active listening techniques to develop and maintain rapport.

(f)   Observe the client's non-verbal signals.

(g)   Once you have an overview of the problem recap on the story to the client.

(h)   Use a mixture of probe and closed questions to clarify.

(i)   Take notes at the recapping and clarification stage.

(j)   Give the client a preliminary legal diagnosis of the problem.

(k)   Invite the client to describe what solutions or remedies are hoped for or expected.

(l)   Review possible options with the client.

(m)   Question for further information.

(n)   Explain and discuss fees and billing arrangements.

(o)   Recap, agree follow-up action, by whom and by when.

(p)   After the interview, send a letter confirming the instructions or agreement reached at the meeting.

Chapter Five

Client Care

5.1 PROVIDING PROACTIVE CUSTOMER SERVICE

If you consider what clients complain about most in relation to their dealings with their lawyers, fees and delays seem to top the list regularly. Often complaints arise because the lawyer has failed to explain key issues at the outset or to keep the client sufficiently informed. People, particularly in this country, still do not like discussing money and there is a tendency to avoid discussions which give potentially bad news, like the probable cost of litigation. Yet if you do not give your clients sound information on fees and how much a transaction or action is likely to cost them, you are preventing them from making informed choices. Clients will also want to know how long it will take to solve a problem or execute a transaction. This chapter will examine how to give clients information on fees and some general client care issues.

5.2 DISCUSSING FEES

At an appropriate stage in the interview you must discuss fees. Most firms have their own practices on what information they give clients on fees and when. Some suggestions and advice are given in 5.2.1 to 5.2.3, but check the policy of your firm. There are also Written Professional Standards specifying what information you should give clients on costs. The Solicitors' Act 1974 and the Solicitors'

Remuneration Order 1972 govern charges for contentious and non-contentious business agreements.

It can be a problem deciding when to discuss fees with clients and there are differing views on when you should give information on fees. The guiding principle appears to be: as soon as it is appropriate to do so. Obviously there are times when discussing fees with a client could be insensitive, like immediately after a bereavement or in an emergency application.

It is also often difficult to predict how much it will cost a client to have a matter resolved, particularly in contentious cases. Some lawyers avoid raising the subject at all for fear it will deter clients. They seem to think that if the client does not mention fees, that indicates a lack of interest. Just because clients do not raise the subject does not mean they are not interested. They may think it is your responsibility. Some may be too intimidated. Rather than get into a dispute later over fees, sort it out early on.

5.2.1 Legally aided clients

If you are dealing with a legally aided client, explain how the scheme works and the income limits. You need not give a technical explanation, but clients are entitled to know where they stand. A client with very little money may be extremely concerned about consulting a lawyer, not knowing exactly how much it will cost. Explain how the rates are set and how you are paid according to these rates and the time you spend working on the case. You should also explain the effect of the statutory charge and any possible contribution your client might have to make.

5.2.2 Private paying clients

Clients who are not legally aided will want to know your charge-out rates, the rates of any other person who may be working with you and the likely overall cost. It is virtually impossible to predict exactly how much a transaction or contentious action will cost, since there are so many variables, but you must try. Looked at from the clients' point of view, they want and need to know probable costs. They may have to budget for legal expenses.

The more experienced you are, the easier it is to give clients a rough estimate. Is this matter relatively straightforward? Will you need to brief counsel at some point? If so, you could warn the client of this. If the client is likely to be billed on the basis of your hourly time, have you conducted a similar exercise for another client which might give you some cost parameters? Is there anyone else in the firm with more experience who could give you some advice on probable costs? Can you at least give lower and upper predictions? If the client is likely to be billed on the basis of your hourly time, you could agree that when you have time recorded up to an agreed figure on the file, you will contact the client to discuss progress. There are many ways of handling this difficult problem of costs, which do not involve opting out when the client asks the feared question, or taking refuge behind a lengthy explanation of the difficulty of giving an estimate.

The new Law Society practice rule on fee schedules gives some guidance on giving clients information on costs. Whatever charging system your firm operates, it is essential that the client understands it. Are you asking for a payment on account? If so, have you explained why? Does your firm charge interest on unpaid bills? What settlement period do you give clients?

You could discuss these issues at the first meeting. If not then, there must be a discussion reasonably early in the relationship. You cannot expect to avoid a discussion and then require clients to pay up happily when they receive a bill, even if the matter did go smoothly. It is also wise, when you send your follow-up letter confirming your instructions, to give the client written confirmation on charging.

Try to be flexible over fees with clients. Would they like to receive interim bills? If so, how often, monthly or quarterly? When the client asks for an estimate of likely fees and costs, explain whether this covers any extras like disbursements and VAT. If you are giving an estimate, make it clear to the client that it is an estimate or forecast and not a binding quotation. If the client is still concerned, explore other ways of allaying concerns about large bills. You could agree to bill up to an agreed figure and no further unless the client approves. Offer interim billing as a way of enabling the client to keep a check on fees and costs. If the matter is contentious, make sure that the client understands the rule that 'costs follow the event'.

5.2.3   Information about costs

Keep clients informed about costs. At least every six months clients should be given an update of the approximate cost accumulated so far. Consider sending interim bills, perhaps on a monthly basis. If your firm has changed its charge-out rates, make sure your clients have been told the new rates.

5.3   CLIENT CARE AND POST-INTERVIEW ACTIVITY

Send a follow-up letter to your client after every meeting, confirming in writing what was agreed. It serves as a reminder for both of you and keeps you in contact. It is particularly important after the first interview when you have taken instructions. Confirm the instructions, the advice given and the fee rate. That way your client will have a clear understanding of what was agreed and what to expect, you will both have a record of that agreement and you will have complied with the Law Society's guidelines. It is also worth including the names of other people, like a fee-earner or secretary, who will be able to answer enquiries when you are out of the office.

Firms are now expected to have a complaints handling procedure. Since 1 May 1991, every solicitor must ensure that clients know the name and status of the lawyer conducting the matter or case and any supervising principal. Clients must also be told whom they can approach in the firm if they have a complaint about quality of service. You may wish to include information on the handling of complaints in your initial letter to clients confirming instructions. Alternatively your firm may have its own policy on this. Make sure you are familiar with your firm's complaints-handling procedure.

5.3.1   Keeping clients informed

Clients are entitled to be kept informed not just about fees but also on progress. You have a professional duty to keep your clients informed, to deal promptly with correspondence and to respond to requests for information. Clients get very upset when they feel they have been forgotten or that progress is slower than expected. Tell them about delays and any changes in the conduct of the matter. If there has been no progress, tell the client and explain why. Delays may be quite outside your control but if the client does not know this you may be blamed. 25 per cent of complaints about solicitors concern delays. If you are going on holiday or transferring the case to someone else, let the client know.

Whatever you agreed to do at the last meeting, do it as soon as possible after that meeting and let the client know. That way you will not receive an angry letter or telephone call demanding to know what action there has been. If you are proactive with clients, rather than merely responding to their promptings, you will be creating the conditions for a harmonious relationship.

5.3.2   File reviews

Regularly review the progress of your files. As well as noting advance warnings and deadlines in your diary, a file review means your clients should never feel neglected. It need not necessarily be you who reviews the files. A good secretary or assistant can easily see the last time the client received a progress report, even one which simply says that you are still awaiting a response from the other party. As well as keeping clients happy, taking the initiative gives you more control over your time.

5.3.3   Progress reviews

At the first meeting you should establish how the client wants to be kept updated and informed. Will it be by letter, progress report, telephone call or meeting? To some extent this will be dictated by the rhythm of the client's work or business. A client who loses pay for taking time off work is not going to thank you for arranging a meeting during working hours, whereas a corporate client may prefer this. A client who cannot receive or make telephone calls at work will not appreciate a request to telephone the lawyer. Try to be flexible and match the method of communication to your clients' needs. Your client may not necessarily want a face-to-face meeting to be updated on progress. Some will, often because they know that at least at the meeting you are concentrating on their case. This is not a good reason to hold a meeting.

Before you next propose a meeting with the client, ask yourself whether it is really necessary. Would a short telephone call be as or more effective? Would a letter serve instead or do the two of you really need to meet face-to-face? If you do need a face-to-face meeting, can you prepare the client for the meeting? Do any documents need to be brought along? What points and issues are you proposing to discuss? Prepare, in advance, an agenda or a list of items for discussion. At the same time, send a letter to the client including that list so your client can come to the meeting prepared.

5.3.4 Post assignment reviews

More and more firms are conducting reviews after the conclusion of a major case or matter. A firm which is committed to delivering a high quality service to its clients cannot afford to neglect the views of its clients. Making time to canvass your clients' views on how their problems are handled is an important part of client care.

5.4 SUMMARY

Much of what has been said is fairly obvious. Yet it is surprising how often these basic notions of good practice are not followed. Do not leave it to the client to initiate a discussion on fees, or to ask for an update on progress. Take the initiative on matters which are likely to be of concern.

5.4.1 Checklist for client care

(a)   Get the fee structure out of the way as soon as possible.

(b)   Don't forget the 'hidden' extras.

(c)   Update your client regularly.

(d)   Is this meeting really necessary or would a letter or telephone call suffice?

(e)   Always confirm instructions in writing.

(f)   Update the file as soon as possible.

(g)   Do not delay

Chapter Six

Attending Behaviour

6.1 UNDERSTANDING NON-VERBAL COMMUNICATION

To make an interview truly two-way you need to establish common ground with the client. Obviously the words and language you use are important. Yet we derive meaning, not just from the content of words but also from how they are spoken and the facial expressions, movements and gestures which accompany them. Some experts maintain that when we derive meaning, we attribute a mere 20 to 30 per cent to the content and the rest to how the words are spoken. This includes tone of voice, pauses and breathing, facial expressions, movements and gestures. It is worth learning about the non-verbal dimension of communication. It has a bearing on how you appear to others and may influence their responses to you. Similarly, considering another person's non-verbal communication opens up a further channel of communication. This chapter will look at how these factors can influence the conduct of an interview.

6.2 BEHAVIOUR

We read and react to other people's behaviour. Bodily contact, proximity, appearance, posture, facial expressions and tone of voice all influence us. There are even more factors which may affect our behaviour. Our image of another person, how senior or junior to us, the occasion, our expectations of that occasion and our own self-image affect how we conduct ourselves. If you are about to go to a difficult meeting with a client who is forceful, sarcastic and senior to you, it will affect your confidence. More important, your lack of confidence may reveal itself in many tell-tale ways without you even realising.

People's impressions, particularly first impressions, are based on the behaviour they see. The signals you send through your behaviour are important because they will have a bearing on how others react to you. Behaviour breeds behaviour. If your behaviour suggests that you are a warm, welcoming person, because you use open-handed gestures, your body posture is open and you use a lot of eye contact, people are more likely to respond to you positively. If you appear defensive, with your arms crossed, shoulders slumped, with little eye contact they will subconsciously read your behaviour as defensive and respond to you accordingly. The same applies to your clients, their reading of you and yours of them.

We were all born with simple reflexes. Gradually, as we matured, we adopted patterns of behaviour which helped us to succeed in certain social situations. We learned to abandon patterns of behaviour which were not rewarded. As people become more experienced in their social and business dealings, there is a tendency to think we know all there is to know about dealing with others. We may also think less about the effects of our behaviour. It is a good thing to become less self-conscious, but a mistake not to pay attention to non-verbal behaviour. By observing the behaviour of others and arranging and controlling your own, you can exercise a positive influence on the interview.

6.3 NON-VERBAL BEHAVIOUR

Verbal and non-verbal behaviour go together and both are observable. When people first meet, a lot of information is exchanged through appearance, clothes, posture, handshakes and facial expressions. In fact, so much information is received and interpreted at that first meeting that this may explain why it is often hard to take in names as well.

Non-verbal communication can play a large part in understanding interpersonal situations. Because it involves a whole range of bodily cues it conveys a lot of information, much of it conscious and obvious and some subtle and unconscious. Its importance should not be underestimated. We need to learn to exercise control over our own non-verbal signals if we want to communicate clearly and persuasively. We also need to learn to 'read' other people. When we receive conflicting messages from people with whom we are in face-to-face communication, the non-verbal cues can override the verbal.

We communicate all the time through body language. How we are being 'read' may not be the message we intend to send. Similarly, we react to others on the basis of their body language, without necessarily appreciating where our reactions come from. If you find someone pushy, friendly, or superior without understanding why, it could be a reaction to their body language. People do make judgments based on non-verbal behaviour. The benefit of being alert to this added dimension of communication is that it gives you extra information. Non-verbal communication is also more difficult to control or choose than actual words.

Communicating behaviour includes:

    (a)   facial expressions, including eye movements;

    (b)   hand and arm movements;

    (c)   leg and feet movements;

    (d)   body posture;

    (e)   spatial distance and orientation;

    (f)   voice pace and intonation;

    (g)   words and use of language.

You can learn how to display positive non-verbal behaviour which has a beneficial effect, and to avoid behaviour which has a negative effect. It takes time and practice to develop these skills and it is important not to make instant decisions. Non-verbal behaviour is easy to observe but difficult to interpret. Simply because someone is sitting with their arms crossed does not necessarily mean that they are feeling defensive or resistant to what you are saying. It may be that he is feeling cold, or that it is the way she always sits. It is the totality of gestures which illustrates behaviour, rather than individual actions. Observe the total body posture, angle of seating or stance, hand, arm and leg gestures and facial expressions. Does the cluster of gestures match what the person is saying?

If a client is saying that he feels quite happy talking about a particular subject, whereas in fact he is hunched up, avoiding your eyes and leaning away from you, you might deduce that he really is not happy. This is not a cue for you to start cross-questioning, but to use a combination of active listening techniques and open questions to try to learn more.

The same applies to your own non-verbal behaviour. If you are feeling ill at ease, angry, impatient or bored, you may imagine that you are concealing these feelings but the chances are that you are not. Some people are better actors than others but we often 'intuitively' know whether someone is concealing something. This is probably from subconsciously 'reading' the non-verbal communication.

Given that we can reveal feelings indirectly, is it then possible to conceal our own irritation, anger or boredom? Up to a point you can. Start by examining the situation or the person. Try to separate what that person is saying from how it is being said, since that may be the problem. Is the person standing too close? Is the eye contact too intrusive or direct?

Learn to be aware of your own non-verbal communication and consciously use open-handed gestures and an open body posture to put the client at ease. Consciously adopting an open posture will also make you feel more at ease and relaxed. Conversely, if you are feeling uncomfortable in a situation, allowing your body to display and experience that discomfort will reinforce your negative feelings. When you are faced with a difficult situation, make a conscious and deliberate effort to adopt a positive mode. It will help you feel better.

Use non-verbal communication to help you establish rapport with your clients. Once you have achieved a good two-way exchange, you should not need to worry much about the non-verbal dimension, apart from checking from time to time that the client's gestures and words are congruent. Congruent gestures are those which are compatible with what a person is saying. If a person is looking uncomfortable or angry but smiling, the gestures are incongruent.

6.4   EYE CONTACT

People pay most attention to facial expressions, gestures and eye contact and least to body posture and leg movements. Eye contact and gaze are the most significant of non-verbal behaviours. The amount of eye contact we give is an indication of the importance we attach to that person and what is being said. If you are trying to influence someone, you will look at that person often, trying to make eye contact and to ensure that you are being noticed. You should be able to judge how the exchange is going between you and your client, partly by the amount of eye contact. Equally, your client will partly be judging you on your body language, including your eye contact.

In Western conversation eye contact is generally maintained for 70 per cent of the time. Any more and that person is likely to be regarded as aggressive and domineering; any less as weak and unconfident. The rate of blinking, dilation and contraction of the pupils and raised eyebrows also gives clues. Apply that to your own interactions with a client: if you look at the client for only 30 per cent of the time, your client may well interpret your behaviour as cold, indifferent or evasive. If your client only looks at you for 30 per cent of the time, you may interpret that as evasion, defensiveness or sensitivity.

Someone who is listening to another is likely to spend more time looking at the other person, typically for 75 per cent of the time, so when you are listening to a client, if you are not looking, the client may subconsciously assume that you are not paying attention. Train yourself to use positive eye contact and congruent gestures to give a good impression. If you are taking notes in the interview, remember that note-taking can interfere with eye contact. Look up as much as possible to show the client that you are giving your full attention.

A person talking may only look at the listener for 40 per cent of the time. A 'look' is generally about three seconds long. Any longer in our culture is interpreted as staring. The French, Italians and Spanish tend to look at people for longer and this is sometimes interpreted by the British as a stare and therefore rude. For other societies, like the Japanese, the British norm of 70 per cent eye contact in conversation is offensive and intrusive, whereas Latin societies regard it as unsatisfactorily low and even offhand.

If eye contact is overdone, for example, if you look intensely or for too long, it can make the other person feel threatened, intruded upon or uncomfortable. If people find you threatening or overbearing, it may be that what you regard as your frank and direct gaze is in fact too intrusive. If you want to soften your gaze, rather than looking straight into that person's eyes, concentrate on the triangle formed by the eyebrows and halfway down the bridge of the nose. Moving your gaze around that triangle (not too much otherwise you will appear shifty) will enable you to look towards that person's eyes but not in a piercing or uncomfortable fashion.

6.5 PROXIMITY

Proxemics is the study of spatial relationships. The amount of personal space we require is determined both culturally and according to our status and relationship to other people. There are considerable cultural differences in spatial relationships. In the West, between two and four feet is about the right distance from another person to create a good working relationship. In the Middle East, this would be considered too far and too impersonal. If you stand or sit closer than two feet to someone in Britain, unless you are on very friendly terms, that person may feel uncomfortable. You will have invaded their 'intimate' space.

How close you stand or sit to someone and the angle of seating or stance will have a bearing on communication in the interview. In 4.4.1 we looked at the importance of seating arrangements in the interview room. Bodily contact is also significant. Friendly touching is associated with liking but if that touching is inappropriate, by touching the wrong part of the body or touching before rapport has been properly established, it will be regarded as an intrusion by the recipient. Similarly, not touching, for example, not shaking hands when it is expected, may be viewed by another as a rejection.

6.6 VOCAL SIGNALLING

Meaning is derived not only from words, gestures and expressions, but also from the voice. How we vocalise, the sounds and noises we make, the intonation, volume, pitch, pace and emphasis can all affect meaning.

Even if you are not all that familiar with your client's voice, you can train yourself to listen for changes in pitch, pace and breathing. Fast, irregular breathing may suggest that the client feels anxious talking about a particular topic. This is a cue to alter your style or emphasis of questioning, or perhaps to probe more deeply. If a client is saying that she feels happy about a proposal but her gestures and tone of voice are not congruent with her words, rather than taking that statement at face value, use active listening and questions to check.

Similarly, your tone of voice will have an effect on your clients. Using a flat, unemotional tone will not put the client at ease. Clients will listen to and read your tone of voice when you give advice or suggest courses of action.

6.7 SUMMARY

There are many cultural differences in non-verbal behaviour. In some countries, shaking your head from left to right, a negative gesture in our culture, is treated as agreement. An up-and-down head shake in our culture means yes, whereas the contrary may be the case elsewhere. This simply serves to emphasise the importance of not leaping to conclusions but using non-verbal communication as part of the interactive process.

Some people have too high an expectation of what non-verbal communication can offer. Others hold the opposite view and claim that this kind of information is trivial. In fact, whether you nodded your head in agreement with the client at the interview may sound trivial but it could have made a huge difference to a client who interpreted this as an encouraging gesture.

Exploring non-verbal communication should not generate self-consciousness. Nor is it unethical to try to control your own non-verbal communication and influence someone else's, provided you are choosing behaviour which assists or enhances interaction. Indeed, you can use the mirroring technique described in 7.5 to put clients at ease. If, in your dealings with others, you adopt an open, relaxed and friendly body posture, the chances are that natural gestures and appropriate bodily contact will develop automatically. If you detect some sort of barrier in the communication process, it is worthwhile exploring the non-verbal dimension, both yours and your client's.

6.7.1   Gestures and possible interpretations

The following lists are signals of differing attitudes. Do not view these in isolation but consider whole clusters of gestures.

Receptiveness or open body posture

(a)   If seated, leaning slightly forward.

(b)   Unbuttoned jacket.

(c)   Legs or feet slightly apart.

(d)   Hands visible, palms turned slightly upwards.

(e)   Comfortable eye contact.

(f)   Nodding gently as the other person is speaking.

(g)   Smiling.

(h)   Hand to face occasionally.

Confidence

(a)   Looking into the other's face (e.g., eye contact for at least 50 per cent of the time).

(b)   Each gaze lasting at least 2 seconds.

(c)   Not much eye blinking.

(d)   Chin thrust forward.

(e)   'Steepling' hands (e.g., fingertips together, fingers pointing upwards or towards listener).

(f)   Little movement.

Defensiveness

(a)   Avoiding eye contact (e.g., less than 15 per cent of time) or looking away shortly after making eye contact.

(b)   Crossed arms, crossed legs, clenched hands.

(c)   Feet pointing towards the door.

(d)   Clenched hands and tight fists.

(e)   Body leaning away.

(f)   Ear, eye or nose rubbing.

Anxiety

(a)   Frequent eye blinking, lip licking, throat clearing.

(b)   Tugging at collar, neck chain, tie.

(c)   Holding hand over mouth while speaking.

(d)   Tugging ears.

(e)   Avoiding eye contact, e.g., for less than 15 per cent of the time.

(f)   Constant shifting of positions or weight.

(g)   Fidgeting, moving around.

(h)   Jigging feet up and down.

Aggressive or overbearing

(a)   Staring.

(b)   Exaggerated expressions of amazement and disbelief.

(c)   Looking over tops of spectacles.

(d)   Raised eyebrows.

(e)   Finger pointing.

(f)   Table thumping.

(g)   Leaning over the other person.

(h)   If seated, leaning back in chair with arms behind head and possibly feet on desk.

(i)   'Steepling'.

Anger

(a)   Rubbing back of neck.

(b)   Jabbing or shaking index finger.

(c)   Scowling, frowning.

(d)   Clenching fists, wringing hands.

(e)   Short exhaling breaths.

Boredom

    (a)   Drooping eyes, blank stare.

    (b)   Straightening then slouching.

    (c)   Head in palm of hands.

    (d)   Crossed arms and legs.

    (e)   Foot kicking or tapping.

    (f)   Wandering gaze.

    (g)   Drumming fingers on table.

    (h)   Body or feet pointing towards the door.

Evaluation or thoughtfulness

    (a)   Slow chin stroking.

    (b)   Pinching bridge of nose.

    (c)   Hand on cheek, often with the index finger pointing upwards.

    (d)   Looking over tops of spectacles.

    (e)   Looking at speaker for at least 60 per cent of time.

    (f)   Head tilted.

    (g)   Leaning forward.

    (h)   Positive body gestures.

6.7.2   Checklist on attending behaviour

    (a)   Be aware of it but not to the point of distraction.

(b)   Make your body language congruent with your words.

(c)   Watch your clients for non-verbal clues.

(d)   Listen to voices and their clues: pauses, breathing, intonation, changes in pace.

(e)   Arrange the seating to suit the client, not just you.

(f)   Use all the information offered by your clients.

Chapter Seven

When Things Go Wrong

7.1   RELOCATING THE COMMON GROUND

So far we have considered ways of encouraging clients to talk, in particular using listening and questioning techniques. Standard techniques will not work with every client. Some clients will be reserved, whereas others may talk too much, be aggressive or overbearing. This chapter selects a range of potentially difficult situations and explores ways of coping.

7.2   YOUR BEHAVIOUR

You should be taking the lead in meetings and interviews. This is not the same as doing all the talking, but clients will inevitably take their cue from you and react to your behaviour. Although you are not responsible for everything that happens, if you feel that the climate in the interview is not right, or has deteriorated, first check out your own behaviour and the signals you are giving.

If you are not looking at a client and do not appear to be listening, you are not creating the right atmosphere. If your body posture radiates lack of confidence or passivity, a client may respond negatively or aggressively. A client wants a lawyer who inspires confidence.

7.3 TOO MUCH TALKING

The client who will not stop talking is likely to make you feel very edgy. You may feel guilty about trying to stop a client who clearly needs to talk to someone. Clients going through a divorce or a bankruptcy may be feeling a strong sense of loss or injustice, which talking can help to ease. It may be necessary, for the first few meetings, to let the client talk. Even though it costs money for you to listen, listening may also give you a clue to what else may be bothering the client. If you let the client talk now, there may be fewer problems later.

Whenever you have a very talkative client, mentally check out your own behaviour. Are you being sufficiently attentive or are you being talked at to gain your attention? Is the client talking to try to divert your attention from some topic where questioning would be unpleasant?

If you have allowed the client to talk or digress for some time and there is no sign of any let-up, the first step is to use a reflective statement which shows that you empathise with the client's concerns. That should then be followed by a suggestion that you both return to discussing the main topic.

> Lawyer: 'I can see that this must be a real worry for you. We can come back to this later but for the moment I should like to continue exploring with you . . .'

If you have tried that approach several times without success, you may need to be more direct.

> Lawyer: 'Can I stop you there for a moment? I would like to go back to where we were discussing . . .'

Or:

> Lawyer: 'Andy, I understand that there are a number of things which are bothering you. However, you initially consulted me about a particular legal problem. I want to help you but until I have all the facts I can't even start to solve it.'

To reinforce your words, consider altering your body posture. As you start to say, 'Can I stop you . . .' raise one hand with the palm vertical, as if you were physically trying to stop the flow of words. Alternatively, if you have been using open-handed gestures, place your palms down on the table and lean forward as you speak. These gestures reinforce the impression of taking control.

Earlier chapters have stressed the importance of eye contact. One way of discouraging the client from talking is to break eye contact. Most people when they talk need a response. If the eye contact, or lack of it, suggests not being listened to, a client may talk less or not at all. Rather than avert your gaze completely, move in and out of eye contact. It is more polite than gazing out of the window, or down at your desk, but still likely to be detected by the client.

If a pattern emerges with a client who rambles or digresses, you may need to abandon your practice of starting the meeting with open questions. Use instead the inverted funnel approach described in chapter 3 and start with closed questions. These will help you to control the pace and direction of the interview. You can always invite open questions later when you have established a degree of control.

7.4   TOO LITTLE TALKING

There are many reasons why a client may be uncommunicative. If a topic is difficult or embarrassing, the client may be trying to avoid it by deliberately changing the subject, or by giving minimal responses to questions. You may have touched upon a delicate topic without realising. If a client has been uncommunicative from the outset, ask yourself whether you allowed sufficient time to establish rapport. Have you phrased your questions in language which the client understands?

Have you have been talking too much and dominating the interview? Contradictory as it may sound, a client may not be speaking now because you talked too much earlier. If you have asked only closed or leading questions, the client may have assumed that all that is expected is to sit back and answer a few questions. If that is what you have 'taught' your client, you may find it difficult to get a response.

When you sense reluctance or lack of cooperation, try using pauses and silences, not pauses to the point of embarrassment, but at least sufficient to show after asking a question, that you are willing to wait for an answer. Consider asking more open questions or, if the problem seems to centre on a particular topic, try rephrasing the question. It is possible that the client genuinely did not understand you and is reluctant to say so.

Alternatively, the client may have understood the question but not its relevance. If the client thinks you are asking about something which is none of your business, you may get no response. Explain the purpose of the question to the client:

> Lawyer: 'I've asked you about your family because I need to know what kind of financial support you will have if you leave your husband. You've said that you don't have much money of your own and you work part-time, so we need to find ways of helping you to cope financially. Will your family be able to help you out with money till we sort out the maintenance?'

As well as indirectly trying to find out what is wrong, you can ask the client directly. If that produces no explanation, consider a follow-up statement explaining why you have asked:

> Lawyer: 'Mr Jones, I had thought things were going quite well. But I've noticed in the last few minutes that you have been rather quiet. Is there anything the matter, anything bothering you?'

If the client started cooperatively, but at some stage in the interview changed, and you suspect it is because the subject-matter is painful or embarrassing, try asking a series of closed questions. Choosing from a limited number of alternative answers may be easier for the client than having to respond to open questions:

> Lawyer: 'Jacqueline, we were talking about when the store detective asked you to go with her to the manager's office. (*pause*) Did she put her hand on you – on your arm or your shoulder? (*pause*) Did she grab you or treat you roughly in any way? (*pause*) Did she say anything to you? (*pause*) What did she say?'

If you think you know why the client has clammed up, use a reflective, leading statement, which suggests what you think is the problem, and invites the client to confirm or deny it:

> Lawyer: 'We've been talking about the day your husband wrote his will. I am sure it must be upsetting to remember that day?'

Perhaps the client is reluctant to talk about something for fear that it may shock you or incur your disapproval. If you suspect that, a reminder that your relationship is one of trust and confidence might help:

> Lawyer: 'When he had been drinking, was there anything in particular which used to upset or frighten you?'

> Client: 'I . . . well, he used to . . . it was terrible really . . . but it only happened when he had been drinking'.

> Lawyer: 'Please don't worry about anything you say to me. I won't be shocked or surprised. It won't go outside these four walls unless you want it to. Our relationship is confidential. But if there is anything your husband did which has a bearing on this, I really need to know about it.'

Use your body posture to reinforce what you are saying to the client. Adopt an open, friendly position, avoid intense eye contact and show you are interested. If you are gazing out of the window, or sitting with your arms folded, or you are doodling or pencil-tapping, you will not encourage the client to open up.

7.5 MIRRORING

You can also use non-verbal communication to reduce tension in an interview or meeting. One technique, known as 'mirroring', is particularly effective for dealing with clients who are uneasy. You may have noticed how people in social situations who are getting on well together subconsciously copy or mirror each other's gestures. They do this without realising.

By consciously following that process of mirroring gestures, you can gradually lead your client into a more relaxed body posture. The technique is often used by professional interviewers and counsellors to put people at ease. It is not a particularly difficult skill to acquire, in fact we all do it subconsciously with close friends. Applying the technique to professional situations simply requires some practice. Practise mirroring, with other people's permission in social or 'safe' situations before you use it in an interview.

The technique operates in three phases: mirror, pace and lead.

Mirror. As you are talking to the client, copy or mirror the gestures. Do not caricature them but present a softened version of the way that person is sitting, what they are doing with their arms and legs and so on. What you are aiming to do is to present a subtle reflection of that body posture.

Pace. Now tune in, not just to the gestures, but also to the rate of breathing and eye blinking. As the client changes position, gradually alter your position to simulate the client's. When you feel that you are properly tuned in to all the movements, move to the third and final stage. You may need to spend several minutes pacing yourself to the other person's movement.

Lead. If you have successfully paced your movements, the other person will subconsciously follow you. Gradually lead, by changing your body posture to an open position. Adopt an open posture, arms uncrossed, palms turned upwards, shoulders back but not braced, good but not threatening eye contact, head perhaps tilted on one side.

You will need to practise mirroring, until the process becomes automatic rather than self-conscious. Once acquired, it is a useful influencing technique for meetings or negotiations, as well as interviews. If you are dealing with someone who is giving negative signals or is being resistant to your ideas or proposals, try the mirror, pace, lead technique as you speak to bring that person round to your point of view. It frequently works. Use non-verbal communication skills to reinforce your verbal skills.

7.6   CLIENT NOT LISTENING

Clients do not always listen to the advice of their lawyers. There are many reasons why you may not be 'heard'. If your advice conflicts with what the client wants to do, with a particular course of action which the client wishes to follow, your client may ignore your advice. Ultimately, it is, of course, the client's decision and choice on proposed courses of action, but it is still your professional responsibility to make sure that your suggestions are considered.

Although it can happen irrespective of your experience, you are more likely to encounter this problem when you are a trainee or a relatively newly qualified lawyer. A corporate client who feels that he or she has been 'fobbed off' with a relatively junior lawyer is capable of making your life a misery by questioning or ignoring your advice. Your comparative or apparent lack of experience, in commercial practice and everyday 'life' problems, lays you open to being disregarded.

Your first response should be to examine your own behaviour. If your demeanour suggests lack of confidence, you may have laid yourself open to this form of intimidation. Check not only your physical non-verbal signals, your body position and stance, but also your voice and choice of language. If your voice sounds timid and you preface your advice with phrases like 'I think', you are more likely to appear unassertive. Using more assertive-sounding phrases like 'What I suggest is . . .' or 'Your options are . . .' will make you sound (and possibly feel) more in control. Consciously adopt some of the assertive gestures listed in chapter 6 to reinforce your words.

If you are confident in the advice you are giving to a client, but you suspect that you are being ignored because of your age or sex, there may come a point at which you may wish to put this to the client direct. Provided you are polite, and present it in terms of a problem to be solved, it could be helpful to the relationship:

Lawyer: 'Mr White, it seems to me that we have reached an impasse. I sense, correct me if I am wrong, that you feel I do not have sufficient experience in this field.

I appreciate that you have more commercial experience of your business. However, one of the advantages of my apparent youth is my up-to-date knowledge of technical legal issues. Together I know we can solve this problem to your satisfaction.'

One final piece of advice. If you find yourself falling into a defensive relationship with a client, start taking steps immediately to reverse the process. Avoid situations which place you on the defensive. Rather than waiting for the client to ring, and possibly harangue you about something you have done or failed to do, keep one step ahead. Always do what you have agreed to do, preferably slightly ahead of time. Take the initiative and ring, or write to the client, giving information on progress, the other side's inactivity, or whatever is contributing to or hindering the conduct of the matter. By taking the initiative you will be better able to exercise control.

7.7 NOT THE WHOLE TRUTH

Often the sensation that the client is withholding or fabricating information is an intuitive one. You may notice that the client has made a conflicting or inconsistent statement or that a statement does not tally with what a witness has said. It may be that you feel that the client's description of events is too far-fetched to be believable. If you think your client is withholding information or making something up, why is that? Is the client trying to avoid appearing foolish? Is the client afraid that if the truth comes out it may affect your view and whether you will continue to handle the case?

If you suspect that your client has concerns about confidentiality, a timely reassurance may clear the air:

Lawyer: 'Can you think of any reason why the police came round to your house?'

Client: 'Not really. They always pick on people like me.'

Lawyer: 'Have they ever done this before?'

Client: 'Once they've got it in for you, they never leave you alone.'

> Lawyer: 'Michael, if you have ever had a brush with the law before, I need to know about it. No one else need know. What you tell me will go no further. But if I am going to defend you in court, I need to know everything there is to know. Do you understand?'

Testing stories for inaccuracies can be difficult. Some lawyers are not very confident with the direct approach of suggesting to a client that he or she may be holding back something important. Instead they use indirect methods to suggest that something is wrong. These range from non-verbal signals indicating disbelief (raised eyebrows, highly interrogative tone of voice), to silence. As a tool to encourage the client to rethink what has just been said, silence can be very effective. Try a face-saving statement followed by silence:

> Lawyer: 'Would you like to change anything you have just said? Sometimes thinking for a little longer can help bring things back.'

If you are convinced that the client is making something up, confronting the client directly can be effective but it is risky. If you are wrong then your client may be very offended. Even if you are right, the client may still deny it. Some people find it hard to admit that they are in the wrong. Alternatively, you may prefer to test your theory in an indirect way before challenging the client's veracity direct. Start by explaining that you are a little puzzled by one or two inconsistencies and draw the client's attention to these. The client's answers may offer some clues for follow-up questions.

Another approach is to put a hypothetical proposition to the client, suggesting that this is what the other side might say and inviting the client to comment:

> Lawyer: 'Mr Smith, you've told me that you never met Mr Arthur in the pub. Mr Arthur says that you did. The police are going to suggest that you deny meeting Mr Arthur because you know you bought stolen goods from him. What would you say to that?'

Of course, you may be faced with a response like 'Well they would say that, wouldn't they?' which would obviously have to be probed further.

A development of the 'hypothetical' is to explain to the client that you are now going to pretend to be the other side's lawyer and 'cross-examine' to get a feeling for the problem. This device enables you to probe at inconsistencies. Playing the cross-examination game with the client should always be accompanied by an explanation that this is just a rehearsal or imitation, otherwise you risk offending the client by your manner.

Without directly suggesting to a client that you think you have not been told the whole truth, you could try recounting the client's version, explaining why you find it difficult to believe. If that fails, you may have to tell the client directly that it is in his or her interest to tell you all the facts so that you can work properly on the case. If your various appeals for clarification or correction have failed, the final option is to refuse to continue to represent the client. Obviously this is very much the last resort, but if you do not have confidence in what the client tells you, that client would be better served by someone else who does.

7.8 DEALING WITH CONFLICT AND AGGRESSION

Occasionally clients may behave in an aggressive or overbearing manner. This behaviour may arise out of feelings of insecurity or anger at being in a particular situation. Sometimes people act aggressively when an issue is very important to them, when they feel confident of their position, or when they feel they have been severely wronged.

Potentially aggressive people need to be handled with great care. The aggression may take the form of being sarcastic or patronising, trying to belittle your efforts, being dismissive of your questions or suggestions, or showing impatience. It is very easy to be drawn into a negative response when faced with an aggressive client. If the client appears to be domineering, larger or more powerful than you, you may feel intimidated or defensive. This could then be reflected in your manner:

Client: 'I don't want to hear any more of this. Why can't you just persuade them to agree? Why do I pay your firm's fees? This problem has been going on now for more than a year. I've been to endless meetings. I've been passed from one lawyer to another in this firm. And now I've ended up with someone young enough to be my daughter.'

If you are not careful, you will fall into a spiral where you are progressively taken less seriously by the client. Alternatively, if you feel equal to the client, you may be tempted to respond in kind, by returning the sarcasm, or reflecting the patronising tone. This is equally unhelpful.

As the professional, you are the one responsible for dealing with the hostility or aggression. Stay calm. Check your non-verbal communication to ensure that you are not sending mixed messages. If you are trying to appear calm but are in fact sitting with folded arms and using a hard or staring gaze, you are responding with hostility. If you are hunched into a defensive position you will appear unconfident. Keep your tone of voice even and low and speak slowly. Speaking quickly makes you sound anxious or ill at ease.

When you have displayed calm and understanding, reflect back to the client the hostile emotion. This shows that you have registered the feeling:

> Client: 'But I want to sue him to teach him a lesson. What the hell is the legal system for, what use are lawyers, if I can't assert my rights?'

> Lawyer: 'I can see that you would want to respond.'

This reflective response must be non-judgmental, to remove the emotion from the response. If it does not, it will just fuel the argument. Avoid the following response which could well provoke a negative reaction:

> Lawyer: 'You may want to use the law for revenge purposes but it is a waste of my time and yours.'

If you are faced with this level of anger, you will have to allow the client to talk. Use active and passive listening techniques in order to dissipate the aggression. Tackle the issues about which the client is complaining, one by one. They may take some unravelling, but do not allow yourself to be rushed, or led into an argument. Do not allow yourself to respond to personal attacks or verbal abuse. Keep the complaints focused on the issues, ask questions, establish the facts and search for solutions.

If it is your first meeting with a client who is being argumentative or antagonistic, until you have established empathy and rapport, it is not a good idea to dive straight in and try to discover the causes for the client's behaviour. Provided the unhappiness has not been caused by your firm, it may be wiser to concentrate on the client interview, deflecting the anger and addressing the legal issues. On the other hand, a quick question could establish whether there is an immediate cause for the client's displeasure, for example, by being kept waiting. If you or your firm are at fault, take responsibility, apologise immediately and clear the matter up. Whether to probe or not is simply a question of experience and judgment.

If the aggression or antagonism emerges at a later stage in the relationship, you must find out why. Get the client to talk in order to diffuse the aggression. When some steam has been vented, use a reflective statement to show that you appreciate that the client is unhappy and that you want to find a solution.

Occasionally, aggression can erupt into bad or provocative language or threats of violence. Although it is rare, if it happens, it can be very upsetting to be on the receiving end. Threats are seldom carried out, but they can cause an atmosphere of violence and make you feel intimidated. If you feel genuinely afraid, use the telephone immediately to call for help, explaining calmly to the client that you would feel more comfortable with a third party in the room. At the same time, continue to speak slowly and calmly to the client to diffuse the aggression. Show that you are calm and self-controlled, but not indifferent. It is hard to continue to be angry with a person who is not. Aim to solve the problem. Gather information, but do not be drawn into an argument, no matter how threatened you feel.

7.9 DEALING WITH HIGHLY DISTRESSED CLIENTS

Clients may arrive at your office in a very distressed state. Alternatively, they may become so in the course of the interview, for example, when recounting traumatic events. It is inevitable that at some time in your career you will be faced with a client who breaks down in your office. You may feel more embarrassed about it than the client.

Do not deny the feeling to the client. It is pointless pretending, by gazing out of the window, that nothing is happening, in the hope that this will give the client some time to recover. Empathise with the stress the client is experiencing and show the client that you are prepared to allow time to recover:

> Lawyer: 'Anne, I'm really sorry we have to go over this. I can understand how upsetting it must be. Take your time. When you are ready we'll talk about it some more. In the meantime, would you like some tea or coffee?'

Modify your questioning style. A series of closed questions may be more helpful to the client and easier to answer.

> Lawyer: 'Let's take this in stages. When did he return?
>
> Did he stay with you for many days?
>
> When did he first hit you?
>
> Did you see a doctor afterwards?
>
> What were your injuries?'

An alternative is to move the questions or discussion to a less distressing subject temporarily. You can always return to the difficult subject when the client is feeling more composed:

> Lawyer: 'George, there are other things we also need to discuss. We can come back to this when you are feeling a little better. For the moment, let's talk about . . .'

You could suggest that the client tries writing down a few thoughts or facts, not there and then but later, before your next meeting. If it is an important but painful topic, the client may find it easier to think and write it down in private at home, where there is less pressure. You can then go through the account with the client at your next meeting.

7.10   EMOTIONAL CONTAGION

Suddenly, in a situation in which you have felt at ease, you may experience a wave of emotion – tension or embarrassment, for example. If this happens, it could be because you have tuned into the client's wavelength so effectively that you are picking up and experiencing some of the anxiety or tension felt by the client. Possibly the client's intense non-verbal communication is affecting you. The first time you experience this it can be very unsettling. Once you have identified the cause, the problem is halfway to being solved. Consciously distance yourself from the emotion and concentrate on the client. Use the standard settling-down techniques of passive and active listening, coupled with careful questioning.

7.11   COUNSELLING

There may come a point with some clients when you feel it is appropriate to refer them for counselling. Before that happens, find out what support groups are available both nationally and in your area. If your office does not have this information, make it your firm's business to collect it. You will be offering a much better service to your clients if you can offer them access to specialised and profes- sional help. This is much better than you feeling you ought to be listening but not really wanting to or being able to.

You should not feel embarrassed about suggesting this kind of professional assistance. Your main professional responsibility is to deal with the client's legal problems. Occasionally you will have to cope with a client's anger or distress. Unless you have been trained, trying to act as a professional counsellor or therapist is exceeding your professional competence. Explain to the client that there are people more qualified than you to deal with this and give the client details of the appropriate agency. If possible, supply also a contact name. You can offer to make an appointment for the client if you feel that would help. If you explain that you need to concentrate your energies and time on resolving the legal issues, the client should not feel ignored or offloaded.

7.12   SUMMARY

The situations described in this chapter and the suggestions offered are clearly not exhaustive. Every client is different and consequently many things will occur in interviews which you will not have anticipated. Being alert, flexible and open is always a good starting-point.

You cannot expect to get on with every client you meet and with whom your work. As you become more experienced, you will develop your own ways of coping. The important thing to remember is that people generally do not act aggressively or unhelpfully for no reason at all. Keeping an open mind, being prepared to try different ways of responding and leading, and concentrating your energies on your client, rather than worrying about your own responses, should help you establish, or re-establish, a good working relationship.

7.12.1   Checklist for dealing with aggression.

(a)   Adopt an open body posture.

(b)   Allow the client to talk.

(c)   Use good listening techniques.

(d)   Focus on issues and facts.

(e)   Avoid being drawn into an argument.

(f)   Do not avoid the aggression – recognise it and bring it out into the open.

(g)   Start a joint exploration for solutions.

Chapter Eight

The Appraisal Process and Interview

8.1 SEEING YOURSELF AS OTHERS SEE YOU

This chapter will explore some of the key features of staff appraisal schemes and how to get the best out of the appraisal process. It will also explore self-appraisal in case your firm has no structured appraisal process of its own.

Although many law firms have introduced, or are currently in the process of introducing, staff appraisal schemes, in reality staff appraisal has always gone on – at least on an informal basis. Wherever you work, you are appraised, evaluated and judged by the people you work with and those to whom you report. As a trainee solicitor your performance and progress will have been reviewed during your articles. You probably received feedback from time to time on your performance. For the fortunate ones, that feedback was timely, specific and built into the training. The less fortunate may have heard only indirectly that a partner was displeased with their performance.

Unsatisfactory as the system of feedback often is in articles, when you qualify you could find yourself receiving even less information. Busy partners often adopt the 'no news is good news' approach to managing their subordinates. You will be told soon enough if you have done something wrong, so if you hear nothing you are expected to know that your performance is satisfactory.

For most people this is not enough. People want and need systematic feedback on their performance. They need to be encouraged and motivated. Organisations also need to monitor performance and train and develop their staff. A good system of appraisal is a useful tool to help an organisation develop standards and motivate staff.

8.2   APPRAISAL SCHEMES

Appraisal schemes have been around in the corporate sector for many years. They masquerade under a variety of titles: performance evaluations, performance reviews, assessment interviews. They experienced something of a revival in the recession in the early 1980s and again in the early 1990s, when some employers saw them as a mechanism for removing unproductive staff. This gave and continues to give staff appraisal a bad name.

There are tremendous benefits to be derived from having a well-structured staff appraisal scheme, both for the fee-earner and the firm. Besides giving partners or supervisors an occasion to discuss performance and achievements, appraisal can be used to clarify the demands of the job or tasks. Ideally, you should receive feedback on your performance frequently and regularly, but if you do not, you should at least be able to rely on receiving feedback at the appraisal interview. The firm appraisal also helps the firm to plan for staff recruitment, training and promotion, to reduce staff turnover and raise staff morale. Improving performance will also lead to increased efficiency and profitability for the firm. If your firm does not have an appraisal system, you can use the self-appraisal system described in 8.6.

8.3   PERFORMANCE STANDARDS AND TARGETS

An effective appraisal scheme needs objective standards against which to appraise. If no standards have been agreed, there can be no real consensus on what level of performance is expected.

A performance standard (sometimes called a performance indicator, objective or quality standard) is simply a yardstick or mechanism against which to measure whether a person is performing to an acceptable level. Standards should be realistic and measurable. Standards relate to tasks and not the individual and they are not always easy to articulate.

For a fee-earner standards might include:

(a)   Recording six chargeable hours a day.

(b)   Completing time sheets accurately.

(c)   Drafting concise and accurate letters.

The job description may lay down standards or at least list specific tasks. Even if your organisation does not have performance or quality standards, it is worthwhile devising some for yourself. At the same time, it is helpful to clarify what amounts to minimal, satisfactory and excellent performance. If you are going to be appraised you can offer these for discussion.

Targets are priorities over and above normal work. They are specific to an individual and are concerned with change and development. They may be remedial, for example, to bring someone's performance up to an acceptable level. They may also be devised to encourage above-average performance or to develop or progress a particular skill. It is important to integrate personal targets and action plans into an appraisal scheme. They are the real basis for future discussions on performance and encourage interest in the job.

Targets could include:

(a)   Attending a training course to develop a new skill.

(b)   Attending more client meetings.

(c)   Recording time more accurately.

Targets make an appraisal system dynamic. They should be set in consultation with the appraisee during the appraisal interview. They should be specific about the end result and the time-scale. Six targets or objectives is the maximum which should be set for an individual.

The current trend is away from linking appraisals to salary reviews, since salary reviews tend to concentrate on past performance at the expense of examining future performance and improvement. The purpose of appraisal is to discuss performance. If the appraisal is linked directly to the salary review, it can reduce the honesty of the discussion and can also confuse the purpose of the appraisal. You may be reluctant to admit to shortcomings in a negotiation over salary. You may try to 'bargain down' future targets to ensure a favourable showing at the next salary review.

Where an appraisal scheme is linked to a salary review, the appraisal should be solidly based on performance, achievements and clearly defined objectives. That way a salary review can be substantiated. Both parties should also be clear on which factors affect salary review and which parts of the process are concerned with career development.

8.4   UNDERSTANDING MOTIVATION

Before you take part in an appraisal interview it helps to have an understanding of some of the theories of motivation. Motivating subordinates is an essential part of any supervisor's role. You and your firm pay a high price for employing demotivated, or under-motivated staff. An awareness of motivation theories may also help you to achieve your outcomes and objectives in the appraisal interview.

All employees, including yourself, have needs and expectations in relation to their work. These vary according to the nature of the job, but at minimum include a pleasant working environment with 'fair' pay and benefits, job security, a degree of job satisfaction, and appropriate and 'fair' supervision. If these are overlooked, employees can become dissatisfied and their performance affected. Motivation derives from the job itself but other factors have a bearing.

Abraham Maslow's theory of motivation is one of the best known. Maslow asserted that every person has a hierarchy of needs and that we all try to progress gradually up this scale of needs, satisfying basic needs and searching for satisfaction of higher-order needs. Maslow offered five levels of need, to be viewed as a kind of pyramid. At the base are level one needs which are essentially physical: the need for food, shelter, sex and safety. Level two needs are concerned with security and stability. Both level one and two needs were described by Maslow as 'lower-order' needs.

People in employment in a buoyant economy are likely to have the lower-order needs more or less satisfied. Levels three, four and five are termed 'higher-order' needs and are concerned with feelings of self-esteem and worth. The need to belong to a family or group, to be accepted, loved and to have good working relationships, all fall within level three (see figure 8.1).

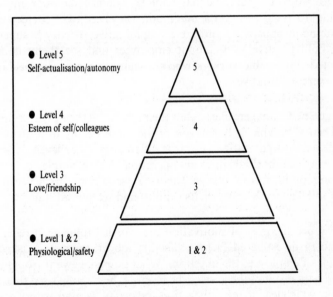

Figure 8.1   Maslow's hierarchy of needs

Level four needs are concerned with self-development, experience and variety. At the top of the pyramid are level five needs: autonomy, the respect of others, self-fulfilment at work and making use of one's talents and abilities.

Maslow's view was that once a need is substantially satisfied, it no longer motivates. Although no needs are ever fully satisfied, if you are a supervisor hoping to motivate a subordinate, you need to discover where that person is on the scale of needs and focus on the one above. If you are about to be appraised, it is worth thinking about your own needs.

A quite different approach to motivation was taken by Douglas McGregor. McGregor posited two quite distinct perspectives on human nature which he called 'Theory X' and 'Theory Y'. He maintained that supervisors or managers tended to one or other of these views in their dealings with their subordinates.

Theory X adherents have a fairly negative approach to their subordinates. They assume that employees do not like work and will attempt to avoid it or do the minimum. They need to be coerced into assuming responsibility and exercising initiative. Theory Y supervisors hold positive views about employees and see them as self-directed, responsible workers, who are willing to accept responsibility and exercise initiative.

Enlightened managers like to view themselves and their organisations as Theory Y typical, but if you probe more deeply into attitudes displayed in organisations towards different types or levels of staff, you may see both theories in operation. For example, it is not uncommon for a firm to hold Theory Y views about its fee-earning staff and Theory X views on its support and secretarial staff.

Two more theories of motivation are worth exploring. Frederick Herzberg investigated factors affecting job attitudes and asked a sample of employees the question, 'What do people want from their jobs?' As a result of the answers he received, he hypothesised that the factors which lead to job satisfaction and dissatisfaction are not equal and opposite.

Certain factors, which Herzberg recognised as motivators, can lead to extreme satisfaction. These include achievement, recognition, responsibility, inherently interesting work and scope for personal development. Other factors, which he called 'hygiene factors', can create dissatisfaction if they exist, but removing these causes of dissatisfaction will not automatically motivate people. Into the hygiene category Herzberg put status, working conditions, salary, relationships with peers and supervisors and the organisation's policies and administrative systems. If an organisation gets these right, its employees may be placated but they will not necessarily be motivated.

According to Herzberg's theory, if you want to motivate your staff you should be aware of the hygiene factors, but you should concentrate your major efforts on offering interesting work, and giving people recognition and a sense of achievement. If you want to motivate people, address their self-esteem and personal growth needs.

Many managers in the 1960s seized on Herzberg's theory because he saw salary as a hygiene, rather than a motivating factor. Subsequent studies on motivation have tended to dispute this low rating for pay. John Stacy Adams explored pay and other factors in his studies on 'inequity in social exchanges'. His 'equity' theory suggests that individuals compare their jobs, status and conditions with their peers, both within and outside the organisation. If individuals feel that they are being treated inequitably, according to their own, possibly selective, criteria, this can affect their motivation.

Space does not permit an in-depth review of motivation theories. Sadly none of these theories derive from studies of human behaviour in law firms. If you are interested in exploring some of these ideas further, there are many books on this topic and some are included in the bibliography.

8.5 THE APPRAISAL INTERVIEW

If your firm already has an appraisal system, it will probably know the stages described in the following paragraphs. What is described is the ideal. If your firm's scheme does not follow the same model, provided it addresses standards, targets and training in a way in which you can contribute equally to the discussion, it is meeting its purpose.

One question which may arise is: who should do the appraising? The logical person is your immediate supervisor, but sometimes that person is not temperamentally suited to conducting appraisals. Your supervising partner may be the kind of person who resents spending time on administration. If so, it may be better to be appraised by another person who has an interest in the process. Suitably prepared, that person should be able to conduct the interview.

There are three main stages:

(a)   Preparation

(b)   Interview

(c)   Review and follow-up

The appraiser should explain the process fully to the appraisee. If you have been appraised before, clearly less time need be spent on this stage. If this is your first review, time should be spent with you discussing the scheme: explaining the purpose, your role in the process, the documentation and the structure of the interview.

This meeting generally takes place at least seven days before the actual interview. The appraiser will need:

(a)   To agree the date and time.

(b)   To go through the documentation which will be used.

(c)   To agree the format of the interview.

The documentation should include, if possible, the job description, performance standards, previous targets and action plans. You should both agree an agenda for discussion at the interview. This agenda and the documentation will form the focus of the interview. Before the interview, review your past performance and consider possible future targets.

The interview is generally in three stages:

(a)   A review of your past performance.

(b)   An assessment of your future needs, set against the background of the firm's needs.

(c)   Target setting for the future and an action plan.

Both parties have a responsibility for the process. The appraiser performs the dual role of considering both the firm's and your needs. You are responsible for identifying areas for personal development and training, and showing how these match the interests of the firm.

The review and follow-up process will depend on the scheme. In an 'open' system, after the notes have been written up by the appraiser, they are given to you to read. If there is a disagreement, a further meeting may be necessary to resolve that difference. Alternatively, you may be offered an opportunity to add your own version to the notes. In a 'closed' system you may not see the appraiser's notes.

Reviewing performance and agreeing targets annually is not the end of the process. Ideally, there should be some mechanism for interim review of those targets, in an informal way, between each appraisal interview.

8.6   SELF-APPRAISAL

What you get out of the appraisal interview will be largely determined by the amount of effort you put into it. A good appraisal scheme will provide scope for you to assess your own performance. This might be before the actual interview takes place, by inviting you to write notes reviewing your performance over the previous year. You might be asked to fill in a form which will be the basis for discussion at the appraisal interview. A third alternative may be simply to ask you to analyse your performance in the face-to-face interview.

When you are assessing your performance it is important to be realistic about your strengths and weaknesses. This is an opportunity to develop action plans for the future, so it is not in your interests to conceal areas where improvements might be made. If you feel that you would benefit from more training on drafting, it would be sensible to discuss this in the appraisal interview and make it one of your targets in your personal action plan, since concealing this from your supervisor will not benefit you in the longer term. Equally, it is foolish to be unduly modest about your good points. If you have particular skills or strengths, these should be recognised and you should be given credit.

When identifying strengths and weaknesses, try to be objective about your working relationships. Do you give clear instructions to people when you delegate? A good test is whether you get your work back in the form you expected. Are you good at taking instructions? Do you manage your time well or do you often leave things to the last minute, creating panics and pressure for yourself?

Client development is also something you should consider. What opportunities have you taken to organise or attend client lunches? How have you assisted the firm's marketing strategy? Have you brought any new clients to the firm, have you cross-sold the firm's services to other clients and have you managed to attract new work from an existing client?

Think about how your personal development can be matched with the firm's needs. Are there growth areas in which you could be involved which would strengthen your position, help your career development and also benefit the firm? Appraisal is a two-way process. Think what you can offer the firm as well as what it can do for you.

If your firm has no system of staff appraisal, you have a choice. You could suggest to your supervisor that you feel you would benefit from this type of discussion and agree a format and guidelines. If this is not an option, you can continue this process of self-appraisal. You will not benefit from the views of others but an annual or six-monthly self-appraisal will at least keep you focused on your career development. Set targets for yourself and review them regularly. Self-appraisal is also explored in *Personal Management Skills* by Stephen Mayson in this series.

Many lawyers neglect career planning, assuming that they will automatically progress up the ladder towards partnership, gradually being given more interesting and demanding work. This is not always the case. When you feel that the time is right for the firm to consider you for partnership, you may find that their views and yours do not coincide.

Chapter 9 explores career planning in more depth. Keep your CV up to date. Keep a record of training courses attended and new skills and technical knowledge acquired. If you are on the Law Society's Continuing Education Scheme, you are required to keep a personal training record. Keep a note of any major projects in which you played a significant part and any client development work. Keep a record of who you supervise, how often and what training, if any, you give.

8.7   TAKING CRITICISM

Despite your best efforts, it is possible that your personal assessment and the appraiser's evaluation will not coincide. You may even be criticised for things you have done or failed to do.

Giving meaningful criticism is a real skill which, if you are fortunate, your appraiser will have acquired. If not, and if the criticism is badly expressed, you are likely to feel defensive and hurt. Sometimes people counter-attack to cover up those feelings. Finding out how other people see us is an important part of self-development but it is not necessarily easy. If your appraiser is not good at giving feedback, you can assist the process.

There are three stages to taking criticism. Listen and repeat it. Rephrase it in your own words, using the active listening technique. Keep an open body posture, keep your self and your voice calm and maintain eye contact. When you are listening to criticism, try to separate what is being said from the person who is saying it. Just because you do not necessarily like being criticised, or the person giving the criticism, does not automatically mean that the comments are invalid.

Then ask the critic to be more specific and, if possible, to give examples:

> Appraiser: 'You never keep clients informed of what you are doing.'

> Appraisee: 'If I understand you, you feel that I could do more to keep clients informed. Could you give me examples of where clients have felt that?'

Keep asking questions in a calm manner until you are absolutely sure that you understand the full extent of the problem. Check your understanding once again by repeating what you have heard and asking for confirmation that you have understood correctly. Once you have clarified the problem, you can either offer a solution or ask the critic for a solution to the problem. The first method is better, since it shows that you have understood and are actively willing to explore solutions, rather than simply responding passively to the criticism.

Everyone has a right to give criticism provided it is well-founded. Equally, once you have found out exactly what the criticism is, you are free to decide what you are going to do about it. Try to avoid defending yourself before you have had time to hear out the criticism. Do not leap in with a denial, a defence or a justification. Do not evade the issue by responding in a 'yes, but . . .' fashion. Do not start an argument because it will only raise the level of tension.

You do not have to agree with the criticism. If you disagree with the problem as expressed, say so in a calm and non-threatening way. If you can give reasons for your disagreement, the other person may then re-evaluate the problem.

There are four stages to receiving criticism:

(a) Adopt an open body posture and listen.

(b) Clarify the problem by asking questions and exploring examples.
(c) Separate the person from what is being said and concentrate on the latter.

(d)   Be receptive to change, offer solutions or ask for suggestions for change.

8.8   YOU AS THE APPRAISER

If your firm does not operate any kind of structured appraisal process and you feel that your secretary or any other staff who report to you might benefit, consider the following questions carefully.

Are you fully committed to doing this? The benefits of a successful appraisal, even as a one-off, are incalculable, but if you are not fully committed to doing the preparatory and follow-up work, as well as the actual interview, you could do a lot of damage. You will have raised expectations without changing very much and this could lower morale. Make sure you allow sufficient time to explain the process. Someone who has never been appraised before may feel anxious or unsure about what to expect.

Ask yourself whether you are properly 'geared-up' to conducting an appraisal interview. An appraisal interview differs from a client interview in some respects although the two types of interview call upon some common skills, such as the ability to listen and to ask open questions. Do you know how to give constructive criticism and effective feedback? Can you be objective? It is quite difficult to be objective about a person's performance when you work closely with that person. Have you considered what will happen if the two of you disagree about performance or standards?

8.8.1   Conducting an appraisal interview

Conducting the appraisal interview is no different from any other interview. Use passive and active listening techniques, ask open questions and try not to dominate the exchange by too much talking. If the appraisee is not willing to open up or discuss strengths and weaknesses, your task will be much harder. If there is a reticence or an inability to reflect on shortcomings, you may have to adopt a more directive approach. If the employee is behaving unusually, try to find out the reasons.

At the preliminary meeting you will have discussed the form of the interview. Wherever possible, try to adhere to that agreed form unless there are good reasons for departing from it. Start by discussing past achievements, taking care to consider not just the most immediate, but the entire year's performance. This applies equally to any discussion about shortcomings. Then discuss standards, where these have been met, not met, or not met as well as you would like. Discuss targets to encourage improved performance. Do not impose targets, but encourage the appraisee to make suggestions, agree targets and an action plan.

Use opportunities to make the interview a conversation, rather than an interrogation of past successes and failures. Find out whether there are reasons for poor or underperformance. Are there any administrative problems? Your secretary or subordinates may shield you from administrative problems but you need to know about them to understand their day-to-day problems. Set short and long-term targets in consultation with the appraisee. Make a note of these and any action plan and when you will meet again to review them. Try to end the interview on a positive note.

The particular skills you need as an appraiser are knowing how to give positive feedback and constructive criticism. They are both essential components of good working relationships but they do not come naturally to most people. It is often much easier to overlook shortcomings, particularly when you work with someone.

If you are in any kind of supervisory role, there will be times when you will have to point out shortcomings. If you do not, you are not actually doing your job properly. You may also be hindering that person's future development and promotion prospects. Your responsibility is to give criticism constructively and effectively so that standards you set are met.

Feedback is information on behaviour and performance. It should be factual and non-judgmental. Any praise or feedback is better than none at all. If you say to someone, 'You are doing a very good job', you will certainly enhance that person's self-esteem and motivation. Even better is to give clear, specific feedback which highlights exactly what that person has done or is doing well.

Appraiser (to secretary): 'I am very pleased with your performance so far. Your documents are well laid-out, there are very few spelling or typing errors and you are punctilious about filing.'

8.8.2 Giving criticism

Criticism should give information on what that person is doing wrong. It is by its nature judgmental. It will inevitably include some degree of subjectivity on the part of the person giving it and it is usually given with a view to bringing about some change on the part of the recipient.

The purpose of constructive criticism is to enable the parties to arrive at a clear and mutual understanding of the problem in objective, factual terms and then work towards a solution. It should be specific and directed towards solving the problem and encouraging improvement. It should concentrate on behaviour or an activity, rather than personality faults or weaknesses.

You have the advantage when you are giving criticism. You have had time to prepare whereas the other person may not be expecting it. The first stage in constructive criticism is to identify the problem. Be as specific as possible. If you feel that someone has an 'attitude problem', and your criticism is expressed in that way it is likely to provoke a negative response. How does that attitude problem translate into practice? Think of examples where problems have actually occurred. Rather than making a general comment on a person's timekeeping, try to be specific about missed appointments or meetings. Try also to avoid subjective and contentious remarks about personality and opinions.

You must also be clear in your own mind exactly what result you want to achieve. How do you want that person to change his or her behaviour? How much change is realistic? If you cannot be clear about the changes you want, it probably means that you have not clarified the problem sufficiently. You then run the risk of making general statements which could produce a counter-attack.

There may be non-work factors of which you are unaware, which are affecting that person's conduct or behaviour. They may be doing a task in a particular way because that is the way they were taught. Try to be open to changing your views during the discussion, even though your objections to the actions may remain the same.

Time your criticism carefully. There is no point in starting to criticise someone at the end of the appraisal interview. If things go badly you will both be left feeling uncomfortable and dissatisfied. Try to end the appraisal on a positive note. If you feel that the person is not capable of making the necessary changes and would be happier in a different firm, do not get drawn too deeply into this kind of discussion. The appraisal interview is not the place to hand out the P45.

Constructive criticism is directed toward solving a problem and facilitating improvement. Because it is specific and concentrates on behaviour or an activity, rather than personality flaws, it is an essential training tool which can work to the benefit of both parties. Destructive criticism is hurtful, is frequently personal and is therefore counter-productive. If you can acquire the skills of giving and receiving criticism, you stand to gain much more in the appraisal process.

8.9 SUMMARY

The appraisal interview is an important exercise for the employer and the fee-earner. A well-managed appraisal system will help a firm to motivate and reward its workforce successfully. If you are preparing to be appraised, conduct a self-audit of your skills and strengths. Try to identify your weaknesses and any areas which require development. Although it is sometimes difficult to own up to these, if you wish to improve, they will have to be examined.

If you have benefited from being appraised, you may wish to consider appraising anyone who works for or reports to you, like your secretary. Explain the process carefully, structure the interview and apply the same techniques you would apply to any client interview. The one possible difference between the appraisal and a client interview is that you will have to give feedback and possibly criticism. Try to be constructive in your approach and remember, to give criticism, it helps if you know how to take it.

8.9.1 Checklist for giving and receiving constructive criticism

(a)   Establish the right climate.

(b)   Focus on behaviour not personality issues.

(c)   Adopt an open body posture.

(d)   State the problem in specific terms – fact and behaviour only.

(e)   Give or ask for examples.

(f)   Use the opportunity to develop and strengthen the relationship.

(g)   Ask for or give solutions or actions for change.

(h)   Gain or give commitment to change.

Chapter Nine

The Recruitment Interview

9.1 MATCHING PEOPLE TO POSITIONS

This chapter is addressed primarily to the qualified solicitor who is looking for a position or intending to change firms. It will explore the whole recruitment process: job search, preparing a curriculum vitae and recruitment interviewing.

9.2 CAREER PLANNING

In chapter 8 there is a section on self-appraisal (8.6). This should be a continuous process. Take a long-term perspective on your career. The *Concise Oxford Dictionary*, 8th ed., defines career as 'one's advancement through life, especially in a profession'. It is your responsibility, not the firm's, to plan and manage it. If partnership is your ultimate goal, do not assume that you will automatically progress up some invisible ladder towards that Holy Grail. In the past it may have worked that way but as things become more competitive, you will have to manage your career progression. Your career is too important to leave to external forces to make it happen.

9.3   SELF-AUDIT

When you are reviewing and setting career goals, a useful starting point is a self-audit. You will not be including most of this information in your final CV but conducting the exercise is essential research.

Life history

Write down brief details about your life before you went to work. This should not just include educational experiences and attainments but also hobbies and activities you enjoyed. You are aiming to develop a biography which will show you how you have developed over time and to identify any particular interests or themes.

Work

In chronological order, list all the jobs you have held, including holiday jobs. If you can remember, include details like salary, start and finish dates and job title. Try also to remember why you took each job, what drew you to it and whether or not you enjoyed it.

Achievements

List all your achievements, not just those which relate to work. These should be successes or activities about which you are particularly proud. Describe in detail no more than eight, three of which should relate to work. You will not necessarily be including achievements on your job application, unless a potential employer asks a specific question on achievements on the application form, but you may be asked a question in an interview on your achievements. Having a picture of your successes will help you to write a positive CV.

Skills

Many people have difficulty in realistically evaluating their skills, often because they are not sufficiently analytical. If you think you have good meetings skills, how do these subdivide? Are you good at putting clients at ease, leading a discussion, reaching agreement, bargaining hard? Analyse the subskills under the broad category and realistically appraise yourself against the list. You may also have skills which are not currently used in a work context, such as driving or foreign languages.

Weaknesses and limitations

In the same way that you should be realistic about your strengths, achievements and skills, you should aim to know what your weaknesses are. You can work on your weaknesses, minimise them, even turn them into strengths but only if you know what they are. What other factors might have had, or may have, a limiting effect on your career? Do you have all the qualifications you need?

Aspirations and goals

You will only be happy at work if your personal goals and values match, or at least are in harmony with, those of the organisation. The previous chapter examined some possible motivating factors. What is important to you: status, routine, excitement, challenge, power, helping others, money? Think about what motivates you and also what your personal values are. If your top values are not in line with those of the organisation employing you, you are likely to be unhappy at work and you will not give of your best.

9.4   CURRICULUM VITAE

Even if you are not intending to look for a new position in the immediate future, always have a draft CV. Update it regularly, at least every six months. As you update your CV, note important or unusual tasks or meetings, major projects, whether you supervise others and ways in which you have been able to exercise initiative or demonstrate creativity. You will not necessarily include all this information in your final CV, but if you keep it on file, you will not forget any essential details. Another approach is to start a personal file. Each time you do something significant, make a note on the file.

9.5   PERSONAL TRAINING PLANS

Use the continuing education scheme to support your career development. If your firm has an appraisal system, your training needs should be addressed in the appraisal interview. If there is no formal or informal appraisal you will have to develop your own personal training plan.

Pick a point in the future, for example, three years ahead and think about what you hope to be doing then. Try to visualise yourself. Realistically, what position do you see yourself occupying? What would you like to be doing? Then work back from there and try to identify the skills and knowledge you will need to help you to reach that point. If you see yourself doing European work, do you have the necessary language skills? If not, what steps are you going to take now, next year and the following year, to acquire them? If you wish to specialise in litigation, do you have the necessary technical knowledge? Do you need to know more about employment or immigration law, social security or tax? If so, plan how you are going to acquire that knowledge in stages.

The continuing education system can be used to support your personal development. In fact, that is how it should be used: to help you acquire or develop skills and knowledge, rather than a frantic scramble each year for two one-day courses, each carrying eight continuing education points. Even though you are likely to be under pressure during your working day, you must also find time to read around your subject and areas of interest. Try to make time each week to do this.

Career planning also entails observing other people's successors. Who is 'on the up' in your firm and why are they successful? Without suggesting you model yourself directly on other people, at least have an understanding of what is valued in your organisation. It is your choice whether you wish to conform. Keep yourself informed of developments in the profession as a whole and maintain contact with your peers in other firms. They may be a useful source of information when you are planning to change firms. Joining groups like the Young Solicitors Group or the European Lawyers Group will also help you to extend your range of contacts and access to information.

You cannot afford to let your career drift aimlessly. It will develop if you create the right conditions for that development, but it is your responsibility. Develop a personal training plan for the next three to five years and work to it. You may need to modify it from time to time but it will be an invaluable aid.

9.6 LOOKING FOR A NEW POSITION

There are a number of options. You can use a recruitment agency or you can go it alone. If you choose the latter, try scanning the specialist legal pages of national newspapers, legal journals, or even sending a speculative letter and CV to a firm. Sometimes asking amongst your contacts in other firms may produce valuable leads. You may even be approached by head hunters, although this search method is generally only used by firms looking for senior staff, or where there is a definite shortage of specialists in a particular field.

9.6.1 Advertisements

Not all firms advertise vacancies. It can be expensive to advertise. It is also difficult, in a few lines, to be explicit about the firm's needs. Consequently, advertisements often use very general descriptions like 'two-year qualified lawyer with a broad experience of commercial property'. This advertisement says little about the precise experience or level of skill required. It will probably attract a wide variety of responses, not necessarily all suitable for the position. Do not feel disappointed if your response is unsuccessful. Often the advertisement and follow-up details give insufficient information to enable you to target your application.

Job advertisements sometimes have secondary purposes. Firms may use recruitment advertising for public relations purposes, to signal their strength in a legal field, or their expansion into new developments. The attraction to a firm of placing a national advertisement is that it may attract well-qualified applicants who are dissatisfied with their current positions, but who have so far taken no active steps.

If responding to advertisements is your main search strategy, remember that there are cyclical peaks and troughs. Holiday seasons are not good times to be looking for a new position. At the start of a new year or after the holiday season tends to be better.

9.6.2 Using a recruitment agency

There was a huge growth in recruitment agencies in the 1980s. It remains to be seen how many survive. Some concentrate on selected specialisms; others cover all fields.

A consultant from a good recruitment agency will have visited the firm and met the partners or administrative staff responsible for recruitment. The agency should have been given general information about the firm and how its recruitment procedures operate. It should also expect to be provided with a job specification, details of the salary and benefits package and a candidate profile. This profile should describe the sort of person the firm is looking for, both in terms of experience and personality. Depending on the seniority of the post, the firm may also give an indication of partnership prospects for the successful applicant.

A firm may use a recruitment agency in a number of ways. It may place an advertisement in the national or legal press and invite responses to the agency. That way the firm need not be named in the advertisement. The agency's role in the recruitment process depends on the arrangement it has made with the firm. It may simply collate responses, prepare a list of candidates and present that list to the client firm. The firm then decides who to select and interview. Using an agency in this way preserves the firm's anonymity and enables it to pass on the administrative burden of collating and processing responses.

Additionally, the agency may have been asked to screen candidates for the firm. If so, it will study CVs and applications and prepare a shortlist. The recruitment consultant may conduct a preliminary sifting interview and may sit in on the interviews in the firm. Finally, rather than advertise, a firm may circulate details of a position to one or more recruitment agencies to find suitable candidates.

If you have not seen any suitable positions advertised, you may decide to approach a recruitment agency. Do not be tempted to sign up with many agencies; one or two should be sufficient. You will be interviewed by a consultant. That consultant performs a dual role: assessing whether you are the right material for the client firm and establishing your experience and potential. If you have already prepared a CV, this will be discussed at the interview. If not, a CV will be drafted with you and with your consent, circulated to the agency's client firms. It is important that you discuss with the consultant which firms you wish to be contacted and in order of priority. If you have a preference for a particular firm, say so.

If you are applying for a particular position, find out as much as possible from the consultant about the position. Explore how your experience matches the job description or details. Unfortunately many law firms still have a lot to learn about preparing a good job description. A good description will specify particular tasks, roles and responsibilities which the fee-earner is expected to undertake or assume. Often descriptions simply ask for experience in terms of years, for example, '18 months' to two years' post-qualification sound experience in commercial litigation'. How will the firm evaluate 'sound experience'? What tasks will the fee-earner take on, how much responsibility will be delegated and what supervision will be given?

As a prospective candidate you should also try to find out how the firm organises its work internally. Are there interest groups or transaction teams? What sorts of training and supervision are offered? Obviously these questions can also be asked at the interview, but the more you know about a firm in advance, the better able you are to assess whether you wish to pursue your application.

9.6.3 Preparing a curriculum vitae

A CV is very important. You will invest a lot of time and energy in preparing your CV. Unfortunately, the attention it receives will not necessarily be commensurate with your effort. It must also pass many tests. CVs are often used to screen people out, rather than screen them in. Your CV must, therefore, appeal to as many people as possible and must be easy to read.

It should contain some quite basic information:

(a)   Personal details: date of birth, address etc.

(b)   Secondary education: number of O levels, A levels and grades.

(c)   Further or higher education: class of degree and college, professional qualifications.

(d)   Employment record: starting with the most recent, list responsibilities.

(e)   Achievements: any particular successes, positions of responsibility at school or college, other achievements.

(f)   Additional skills: language skills, a clean driving licence etc.

(g)   Other information: outside work interests.

Anything which distinguishes you positively from other candidates is important. If you are asked at this stage to provide names and professional referees, make sure you have asked your referees if they are willing to act.

A useful starting-point when drafting a CV is your current or last position. Write it down, together with a short, descriptive paragraph of your general duties. Reread that paragraph. What are the two or three most important tasks or transactions you work on? List the skills which you employ for these. List the achievements which relate to these. For example, you may have played a significant part in a large commercial property development. Besides helping to resolve legal problems and using research skills, you will have used other skills. You may have taken part in negotiations or helped to arrange the finance. Think about your role in the project and what you contributed. If you handle a large case-load with little supervision, what skills does that require? What have you done in a work context of which you are proud?

The potential employer is most interested in achievements as this is what distinguishes you from other applicants. Do not exaggerate your achievements but use them to demonstrate your ability to work well with other people. Imagine that you are preparing for a salary review with your current firm. What achievements would you wish to

discuss? List these in outline. If you are still having difficulty, think
back to a recent problem you tackled at work and how you solved it.
Then consider the results of your solution in terms of how your efforts
benefited your firm.

Another helpful exercise is to think about other fee-earners or
employees in your firm who have not been successful. What did they
do wrong? What did they do differently from more successful
fee-earners? In comparison, what are you good at? An employer is
looking for positive attributes which make you a desirable fee-earner.
Unless you can identify these, either in your CV or at least during the
interview, you will not be offered the position. Preparing a CV is stage
one of projecting yourself successfully in the interview. Potential
employers are also looking nowadays for people who are efficiency
minded, profit orientated, and highly committed to clients and
solving their problems. Think back over your work history and
identify ways in which you can illustrate those attributes.

You can present your CV in a number of ways. One is to give
chronological data about your employment. Start with your current
or most recent position and then work backwards. Another is to
prioritise jobs and work experience, starting with the most senior or
significant position and working backwards. Often the two will lead
to the same order of information but not necessarily. During your
articles, the most interesting or significant work you were given may
not necessarily have matched your experience. Sometimes it was
fortuitous. If, in your third seat in the commercial department, you
were closely involved in a major contested takeover, and you are now
applying for a position in corporate work, you will give that
experience prominance. If you are applying to practice in the
employment field, collect together all your previous experience on
your CV. A prioritised CV emphasises your most relevant experience
to the potential job position.

If the firm has prepared a useful job description, you could consider
sending with your CV an 'executive briefing'. To prepare an executive
briefing, draw a line down the middle of a sheet of paper. On the
left-hand side list the particular tasks, skills and responsibilities which
the firm has specified. On the right-hand side list your skills and how
these match the requirements of the firm. Going to this effort can

substantially increase your chances of obtaining an interview. It shows that you have thought about the position and can offer a perspective on how to carry out those tasks and responsibilities.

Try to keep your CV to a maximum of two pages. Emphasise your achievements and problem-solving skills but do not try to include everything. Leave something to discuss at the interview.

9.7 PREPARING FOR THE INTERVIEW

If you are using a recruitment agency they should have given you the necessary information about the firm, its reputation, training policies, full details of the position and who will be conducting the interview. If you are going it alone, find out as much as you possibly can. Study the firm's brochure and any other literature about or published by, the firm, which might give you an insight into its activities. Make a list of the key points you wish to put across at the interview. You will have to sell yourself and your skills. Interviewers recognise that they have a responsibility to draw candidates out but you must be able to take every opportunity offered to perform well. As well as identifying your strong points, face up to potential weaknesses. How will you respond to questions on these? Can you prepare answers which are credible?

You should not lie in a recruitment interview. On the other hand, telling the plain truth may not help you. If you loathed your six-month seat in articles in litigation, rather than admit to that, say that you preferred another department because of the wider experience you gained.

The benefits of practising for the interview cannot be overemphasized. Devise a number of potentially tricky questions which you would not like to be asked. Work out answers. Practise saying those answers aloud. At first you will feel awkward but it will gradually become easier. Practise aloud answers to potentially helpful questions like: Why do you want the position? What do you have to offer? Learn to describe your previous experience in a succinct and interesting fashion. Do not worry about overrehearsing or sounding as if you have learned your lines. It is very unlikely that you will sound that way at the interview.

During the interview you are likely to be asked many searching questions which are designed to test your confidence, experience, and ability to fit in the firm. Some of these questions may try to trick you into contradicting yourself. Others may be designed to probe how well you react under pressure. Basically, your potential employer is trying to find out four things:

(a)   Can you do the job?

(b)   Will you fit in the firm?

(c)   Will you fit into a particular department?

(d)   Is the salary acceptable to you?

Very few of these questions actually relate to your professional skills. Whether you fit will be very important to the firm. The firm may also be looking for someone who will in the future be considered for partnership so they may try to establish whether you are partnership material.

9.7.1   Presentation at the interview

First impressions are the strongest. These will initially be based on your appearance. Dress fairly conservatively. Try not to drink alcohol the day before an interview. It will affect your eyes, your skin and your wits.

Arriving five minutes early for the interview is acceptable. Arriving 25 minutes early shows over-anxiety. Arriving late is unforgivable. Try to arrive about five minutes early to give time to compose yourself and your appearance. Mentally rehearse your key points and the positive statements you wish to make. Breathe deeply and slowly to dispel tension. Keep reminding yourself that you want this job and that you are going to be a success in the interview.

When you first meet the interviewer, try to establish rapport. Shake hands, maintain an even but non-intrusive eye contact and adopt an open body posture. It is the responsibility of the interviewer to put you at ease. If that is not happening, do not show that you feel put out or discouraged. Present yourself as calm and even-tempered. If the seating arrangements are awkward, politely ask if you may move your seat. If there is more than one interviewer, place yourself so that you can address your answers to them all. Avoid the trap of responding only to the person who asks a question.

A good interviewer will have read your CV thoroughly and planned a sequence of questions. Questions about skills and experience may be mixed with questions designed to discover what kind of person you are. In your answers, try to strike a balance between giving useful information about yourself and not boring the interviewer with too much detail.

There are four things you absolutely must avoid:

(a)   Not listening to the question properly.

(b)   Answering a question you were not asked.

(c)   Giving lengthy and verbose answers.

(d)   Not being properly prepared.

Sometimes it is difficult to understand the relevance of the questions you are asked. On other occasions you may be asked searching questions like 'What is your greatest weakness?' and 'What interests you least about this job?' to which no-one would give a totally honest answer. Other questions like 'Why do you want to work here?', 'What particular experience can you offer?' and 'What are your greatest accomplishments?' are easier to answer.

You will be asked questions which test your motivation, drive, commitment and ability to get things done. Your answers should project you as a successful and effective fee-earner. Employers are looking for people who have sufficient self-confidence to conduct themselves in a variety of situations. They are also looking for staff who are reliable, have professional integrity, commitment to doing the job well, good analytical skills and the ability to get on well with clients. They will probably also be looking for someone who can work within the firm's procedures and who will assist their profitability.

Your responses to questions and your ability to project yourself as someone who matches those attributes, will determine how successful you are in the interview. You are unlikely to be strong in all areas, in which case it is important to know when to keep your mouth shut. If a question disturbs your equilibrium, do not assume that you have 'failed' the interview. The question may have been specifically designed to assess how you behave when you are flustered. If you can recover and not appear discouraged, the interviewer is likely to be favourably impressed.

9.7.2   Answers to difficult questions

Use your answers to project yourself as a problem solver, as someone who can work in a team and be organised. Here are some potentially difficult questions you might be asked in an interview:

'Why do you want to work here?'

Respond in terms of how you see the firm's profile and position in the market-place. Imply that the firm has the kind of reputation which you think would encourage your best work. Show by your answer that you have done your research.

'What kind of experience do you have for this job?'

This is an opportunity to sell yourself. If you have gained experience in your previous employment which you think would be of interest, describe it. If not, demonstrate the transferability of your experience.

'Are you well-organised?'

You are expected to demonstrate that you know how to organise your time, that you believe in planning your day and that at the end of the day, you review the day's events and prepare for the following day's activities.

'What did/do you like and dislike about your last job/about your current job?'

Be very careful what you say about your current or previous employer. It is not a good idea to criticise. Keep your answers short and positive. Your reasons for moving should be given in terms of looking for more opportunities in a larger firm, or for a more intimate working environment in a smaller firm, whichever is appropriate.

'How long would you expect to stay with the firm?'
This might indicate that they are thinking of offering you the job. Answer that you are looking for a future with this firm, to grow with them professionally and to develop your career. If this question is asked early in the interview, do not ask then about partnership prospects. Save that question until you have been offered the position.

'How long would it take you to make a contribution to our firm?'

Consider putting this question back to the interviewer as, 'What would you expect my responsibilities to be within the first six months?' This will give you time to think and also to find out whether they want you to start work on a particular matter or whether they are going to give you time to settle in gradually.

'What are your biggest accomplishments?'

The interviewer will be primarily interested in your work-related accomplishments rather than achievements in your personal life. However, if you can show that you have done something of significance outside work, describe it. When you describe your accomplishments at work, strike a balance between those which reflect on you individually and those which illustrate team accomplishments.

'Tell me about yourself.'

Rather than ramble on about yourself, clarify with the questioner what it is he or she wants to know. Does the interviewer want to know about your interests out of work, or what work you have been doing recently? The interviewer may be trying to discover whether you are a team worker, whether you have some particular legal skill or technical expertise to bring to the firm, or whether you are a potentially good project leader. It is always useful to finish your answer with some 'sweeping-up statement' which suggests that you put your best efforts into everything you do.

'Can you work under pressure?'

This is, in fact, not a very good question, being a closed question which can be answered with a simple yes or no. Show that you are able to plan and manage your time to minimise unnecessary pressures and stress, but also that you understand the importance of meeting clients' needs.

'What is your greatest strength?'

The sorts of strengths the interviewer is looking for are reliability, ability to work in a team, dedication to completing projects, ability to work under pressure and to meeting clients' needs.

'What interests you most about this job?'

You need to be absolutely sure, before you answer this, that you fully understand what the job entails. It may be necessary for you first to ask the interviewer a few questions about the job before you commit yourself. If not, you could fall into the trap of not giving a sufficiently full answer. Once you have clarified the demands of the particular position, give an answer which presents you both as a team-player and as self-directed. Try also to include a reference to some of the firm's most recent achievements, or its reputation, and how you are looking forward to making a contribution to its future successes.

'What could you do for us that someone else could not do?'

Once again, do not answer this question until you are absolutely sure you understand what the job entails. Then respond in terms of your commitment, ability to work hard and so on. It might then be sensible to conclude your answer by putting the question back and asking, 'How do these qualities fit your view of the job?' That will give the interviewer an opportunity to respond if you have not covered what was required.

'Describe a difficult problem you have dealt with.'

This is a favourite difficult question. It is intended to test your analytical skills. Give an example of the problem and then your solution, presenting yourself in a way which demonstrates that you are well organised, able to assume responsibility, exercise initiative and yet still work as part of a team.

'What is your greatest weakness?'

This is an invitation for you to damn yourself. The safest thing is to give a very general answer, preferably expressing your so-called weaknesses in terms of positive characteristics. For example, you might suggest that you sometimes find it difficult to understand why other people are not prepared to work as hard as you, why they do not pay as much attention to detail, or completing tasks, as you feel is necessary. If you do talk in terms of detail, take care how you phrase your answer. Lawyers want people who take care over detail, but not at the expense of getting the job done.

'What interests you least about this job?'

There will be something which does not attract you and in fact it would be transparently dishonest to pretend otherwise. Pick on something minor, but also suggest in your answer that you know you will have to take the rough with the smooth. If you have a large number of concerns, perhaps this is not the right job for you.

9.7.3 Questions to ask in the interview

Your questions should demonstrate that you have done your research and have a real interest in the firm. The answers will tell you a lot about the firm, how it sees itself and how it is able to sell itself to you. You might ask about:

(a) Working arrangements: is the firm organised on a departmental basis, in working groups or teams? How is the expertise spread across the firm?

(b) Opportunities: to acquire a new specialism, for training, to support fee-earners on continuing education, to attend external courses?

(c) Support services.

(d)   Involvement in client development: marketing, bringing in new clients, writing publications.

(e)   Supervision and career progress: will you receive feedback on your performance, is there a formal or informal system of appraisal?

9.7.4   Closing the interview

If you failed to make some of your key points effectively, take any opportunity offered at the end of the interview to improve on what you said. End on an up-beat note, showing that you have enjoyed the interview. Even if you feel disappointed by your performance, do not let it show. You are very unlikely to be told at the interview whether or not you will be offered the position. The most you can expect is to be told when you will hear by.

9.7.5   After the interview

Make notes on the interview whilst it is still fresh in your mind. Note the names of the people you met, what aspects went well, less well and why. Make a note also of your understanding of the job and your abilities to meet it. Note what was said during the last few minutes and the agreed next step.

In general commercial life it is not uncommon practice for the interviewee to write a follow-up letter to the interviewer, acknowledging the meeting. This is seldom done in legal circles. If you do decide to do it, show in your letter what impressed you, what you see as the challenges of the job and what you recognise as important. If you are going to send this type of letter, do it within 24 hours of the interview.

9.7.6   Handling rejection

Despite your best efforts, you will not be offered every job for which you are interviewed. If you are turned down, try not to let the rejection upset you. You will look back some day with relief on not joining that particular firm. Jobs are not always given to the right people, but to the most determined people. Practise even harder before the next interview. It is a good idea to have a number of interviews going at the same time so that you can keep up the momentum.

If you are rejected, particularly in person or over the telephone, thank the interviewer for the interview and then ask politely for the reasons why you were not chosen. Listen, do not interrupt, and take notes. Feedback on your performance at the interview is essential if you are to be successful in future interviews. If you have received a rejection letter, you should still consider telephoning and asking why you were not successful.

9.8   CONDUCTING A RECRUITMENT INTERVIEW

This section is comparatively brief. For your first few post-qualification years you are more likely to be on the receiving end of recruitment interviews than actually conducting or assisting in the recruitment process.

If you are involved in the search process, ask the following questions:

(a)   Can the vacancy be filled internally?

(b)   What skills and knowledge are required for the post?

(c)   Which are essential and which could be acquired later by training?

Recruitment interviewing is very time-consuming. The more you clarify and define the tasks and responsibilities of the post, the easier it will be to assess whether candidates meet your requirements.

Manage the recruitment interview as carefully as you would a client interview. Be punctual, create the right environment and atmosphere and appear attentive and interested in what the candidates have to say. Ask open questions which enable candidates to demonstrate their expertise. Use active and passive listening techniques. If a candidate appears ill at ease, consider using the mirroring technique, described in 7.5, to help settle that person down.

Before the interview, prepare a plan of the questions you intend to ask. You will be looking for someone who can do the job and who will fit into the firm and the department. If you are interviewing a number of candidates, try to put the same questions to each candidate. It will help you compare their merits when you have to make a decision.

If you are one of a pair, or panel of interviewers, try to sort out in advance your respective roles. Who will lead the interview? Allocate topics for questioning. Try to present a coordinated approach and not interrupt each other. Agree in advance who will answer the candidate's potential questions about the firm and the position. Are you properly informed about these?

The purpose of the interview is to select the right candidate. That does not mean necessarily selecting the person who makes an instant good impression. First impressions are important, particularly in front-line posts, like receptionist. For many positions, the ability to do the job and work well with colleagues is also what you are looking for, so try to get below the superficial to find out what a candidate is really like.

9.9   SUMMARY

To be successful in interviews you must be in training. Part of that training involves keeping your CV current. Be realistic about your strengths and weaknesses and develop career aims and goals. Presenting yourself well in a recruitment interview is a skill, just like any other. Lawyers, and others who are accustomed to asking the questions in interviews, sometimes find it difficult to adjust to being on the receiving end. If that applies to you, you will have to practise even harder, to create the right impression and sell yourself to the best of your abilities.

9.9.1   Checklist for the recruitment interview

Do:

   (a)   Ask questions about the firm and position.

(b)   Show decisiveness and enthusiasm.

(c)   Use eye contact to include all people on the panel.

(d)   Take opportunities to show how your skills and abilities match the needs of the job.

(e)   Find out if this is the only interview or whether there will be a second interview.

(f)   Leave the interview on a positive note and show that you have enjoyed it.

Don't:

(a)   Discuss salary, vacation and benefits at the first interview.

(b)   Allow yourself to appear discouraged if part of the interview does not go well.

(c)   Press for an early decision. It is better to ask, 'When will I know your decision?'

Bibliography

J. S. Adams, 'Inequity in social exchanges', in *Advances in Experimental Social Psychology* (New York: Academic Press, 1965).

D. Binder and S. Price, *Legal Interviewing and Counselling* (West Publishing, 1977).

W. Bingham and B. V. Moore, *How to Interview*, 3rd ed. (New York: Harper & Brothers, 1941).

D. Bone, *A Practical Guide to Effective Listening* (Kogan Page, 1988).

T. Dell, *How to Motivate People* (Kogan Page, 1988).

A. Dickson, *A Woman in Your Own Right* (Quartet Books, 1982).

R. Fisher and S. Brown, *Getting Together* (Penguin, 1988).

P. Honey, *Face to Face*, 2nd ed. (Gower, 1988).

F. Herzberg, B. Mausner and B. Snyderman, *The Motivation to Work* (New York: John Wiley, 1959).

R. L. Kahn and C. F. Cannell, *The Dynamics of Interviewing* (Wiley Int., 1957).

H. Kindler, *Managing Disagreement Constructively* (Kogan Page, 1988).

K. A. Kovack, 'What motivates employees? Workers and supervisors give different answers', *Business Horizons* (Sept–Oct 1987).

Law Society, *Client Care: A Guide for Solicitors* (1991).

Law Society, *The Guide to the Professional Conduct of Solicitors* (1990).

S. R. Lloyd, *How to Develop Assertiveness* (Kogan Page, 1988).

D. McCann, *How to Influence Others at Work* (Heinemann Professional Publishing, 1989).

D. C. McClelland, *The Achieving Society* (New York: Van Nostrand Rienhold, 1961).

D. McGregor, *The Human Side of Enterprise* (New York: McGraw-Hill, 1960).

I. MacKay, *A Guide to Asking Questions* (BACIE, 1987).

I. MacKay, *A Guide to Listening* (BACIE, 1984).

A. Maslow, *Motivation and Personality* (New York: Harper and Row, 1954).

G. Nierenberg and H. Calero, *How to Read a Person like a Book* (Thorsons, 1980).

A. Pease, *Body Language* (Sheldon Press, 1988).

C. Roberts, *The Interview Game and How It's Played* (BBC, 1985).

C. R. Rogers, *Counselling and Psychotherapy* (Boston: Houghton Mifflin, 1944).

R. Sharpe, *Assert Yourself* (Kogan Page, 1989).

A. Sherr, *A Guide to Interviewing for Lawyers* (Sweet and Maxwell, 1986).

F. Silverman, *Handbook of Professional Conduct for Solicitors* (Butterworths, 1989).

D. R. Stubbs, *Assertiveness at Work* (Pan Books, 1986).